MEN-AT-ARMS SERIES

EDITOR: MARTIN WINDRO

CW00539408

The Spanish Foreign Legion

Text *by* JOHN SCURR
Colour plates by BRYAN FOSTEN

OSPREY PUBLISHING LONDON

Published in 1985 by
Osprey Publishing Ltd
Member company of the George Philip Group
12–14 Long Acre, London WC2E 9LP
© Copyright 1985 Osprey Publishing Ltd

British Library Cataloguing in Publication Data

Scurr, John
   The Spanish Foreign Legion.—(Men-at-arms
   series; no. 161)
   1. Spain. *Ejército. Legión*
   —History
   I. Title   II. Series
   355.3′5   UA789

ISBN 0-85045-571-5

Filmset in Great Britain
Printed in Hong Kong

Author's note

Among many works consulted in the preparation of
this book the author found the following most useful:
La Legión Española, 50 Años de Historia, La Legión,
1970; *Uniformes de la Legión*, Jose Maria Bueno, 1980;
Francisco Franco, un Siglo de España, Ricardo de la
Cierva, 1973; *Diario de una Bandera*, Francisco Franco,
1922; *General Millán Astray*, Carlos de Silva, 1956; and
Yagüe, un Corazón al Rojo, Juan José Calleja, 1963. The
author would like to thank Coronel Diego Martín-
Montalvo y San Gil, Comandante Angel Fernández
and especially General de Brigada Ezequiel Morala
Casaña, all of the Museo del Ejército, Madrid, for
their kind assistance and hospitality.
   To General Morala Casaña, veteran of the Spanish
Civil War and former Colonel commander of a
Tercio of the Legion, this book is respectfully
dedicated.

The Spanish Foreign Legion

The Foundation: October 1920

In a crumbling barracks in the Moroccan city of Ceuta, the officer who had founded the Spanish Foreign Legion stared fixedly at a new recruit.

'Do you know why you have come?' the officer asked. 'You have come to die! Yes, to die! Now that you have crossed the Straits, you have neither mother, sweetheart nor family. From now on the Legion will be all of these to you. Duty must come before everything else, now that you have undertaken the honour of serving Spain and the Legion. There is still time to consider whether you are prepared to make this sacrifice. After thinking it over, you can inform the captain adjutant of your final decision.'

This declaration was typical of the fanatically brave and patriotic Lt.Col. José Millán Astray Terreros, then 41 years old. Having first seen action at the age of 17 while serving in the Philippines campaign of 1896–97, Millán Astray had, since September 1912, spent most of his time in Morocco in command of native troops, most recently with the 2nd *Tabor* (battalion) of *Regulares* of Larache.

In 1904 the French government, while continu-

Comandante Francisco Franco addresses the 1st Bandera of the Legion after landing at the port of Melilla on 24 July 1921, just in time to save the city from Rifian forces advancing after their devastating victory at Annual. (Agencia Efe)

Legionaries of the 1st Bandera after occupying an enemy redoubt at Ras Medua on 21 November 1921. The central figure bears the standard of the 1st Bandera (see Plate A4). To his right is a bugler, shown by the red looped insignia on his lower sleeves. All are armed with M93 Mauser rifles. (Agencia Efe)

ing to encroach westwards into Morocco, agreed that the northern coastal region bordering the Mediterranean would be regarded as a Spanish zone of influence. When French forces occupied Fez in 1911 the Spanish felt obliged to venture forth from their five garrison towns into the hinterland, ostensibly to establish the authority of the Sultan of Morocco over the rebellious *kabyles* (tribes) of Yebala, Gomara and the Rif Mountains; and on 27 November 1912 Spain signed a Protectorate Treaty with the French. Millán Astray became convinced that the fierce tribesmen of the Protectorate could never be successfully pacified by an army of reservists and conscripts. The need for a supremely professional fighting corps drew his attention to France's successful employment of such a force in Algeria and the French zone of Morocco—the French Foreign Legion. After presenting a plan for a Spanish Legion to the Minister of War, Gen. Tovar, Millán Astray was authorised to proceed to

Algeria. There, from 7 to 27 October 1919 at Tlemcen and Sidi bel Abbès, he studied at first hand the organisation, discipline and élan of France's world-famous corps of foreign volunteers.

It was not until 4 September 1920 that a Royal Order finally authorised the formation of three *banderas* (battalions) of the '*Tercio de Extranjeros*'— 'Regiment of Foreigners'. However, in practice it turned out to differ from its French model, in that very few foreigners joined it; and over the years the Spanish composition of the unit remained fairly consistently at 90 per cent. (During the 16th and 17th centuries the invincible regiments of Spanish infantry which had swept all before them in Italy and Flanders had been titled '*tercios*'. This name, however, was never accepted by Millán Astray, who always insisted on calling his creation '*la Legión*', as indeed did all others who served in it.)

After organising recruiting offices in Madrid, Zaragoza, Barcelona and Valencia, Millán Astray proceeded to Ceuta on 11 September to establish his Central Recruiting Office in the King's Barracks. He had already selected as his second-in-command the 27-year-old Comandante (Major) Francisco

Franco Bahamonde. Franco had established a reputation in the army for exceptional courage, coolness and devotion to duty while serving principally with the 1st and 2nd Tabors of Regulares of Melilla and the 1st Tabor of Tetuán. Always at the head of attacks and only wounded once, Franco was said by the Moroccan soldiers under his command to have 'baraka'—divine protection. Delighted by Millán Astray's telegraphed offer, Franco immediately accepted, postponed his intended wedding and, on 10 October, sailed from Algeciras on the trans-Mediterranean ferry boat *Fernández Silvestre*, in charge of the first shipment of recruits.

There were 200 men in this first batch. Some were discharged soldiers from Spanish or other European armies; some were adventurers, and others fugitives from the law, from women or from hunger. When assembled in the courtyard of the King's Barracks in Ceuta the recruits were warmly welcomed to the Legion by Lt.Col. Millán Astray, who nonetheless warned them:

'There will be constant sacrifices. In combat you will defend the most difficult and dangerous posts, and many of you will die. There is nothing finer than to die with honour for the glory of Spain and its army, as you will soon learn.'

The following afternoon, at a fortified barracks to the north-west of Ceuta called Position A, Franco began instructing his 1st Bandera. On 16 October the Bandera marched four miles to Dar Riffien to establish the Legion's depôt and to continue training. At Dar Riffien, within a few years, there would emerge the finest living-quarters, workshops, gardens and recreational facilities in the Spanish army, with a water reservoir piped from a mountain stream, and with fresh meat, vegetables and fruit all raised on the Legion's own farm to supplement meagre army rations. All of this was very much the product of the industrious and meticulous organiser, Comandante Franco.

Batches of recruits continued to arrive from Spain. They were normally aged between 18 and 40, needed no documentation, and could enlist under their own or a false name. An enlistment bounty of 500 pesetas was paid for three years and 700 for five. Daily pay soon became 4 pesetas 10 centimos, considerably higher than in any other Spanish army unit. On 31 October three banderas paraded to swear fidelity to Spain and King Alfonso XIII. The Legion now consisted of Command

Comandante Franco, with officers of his 1st Bandera, directing fire against tribesmen retreating from the redoubt at Ras Medua. (Agencia Efe)

Headquarters, Administrative Headquarters, four Depôt Companies, and the 1st, 2nd and 3rd Banderas, each composed of headquarters, two rifle companies, and one machine gun company with six weapons.

The Legion's Creed

At Dar Riffien, Millán Astray composed the following Credo for the Legion:

The spirit of the legionary: It is unique and without equal, blindly and fiercely combative, seeking always to close in on the enemy with the bayonet.

The spirit of comradeship: With the sacred oath never to abandon a man in the field even if all perish.

The spirit of friendship: Sworn between each two men.

The spirit of unity and succour: At the cry of 'To me the Legion!', wherever they may be, all will go to the rescue and, with or without reason, will defend the legionary who called for aid.

The spirit of marching: A legionary will never say he is tired until he collapses with exhaustion. The corps will be the swiftest and the toughest.

The spirit of endurance and perseverance: He will never complain of fatigue, nor of pain, nor of hunger, nor of thirst, nor of drowsiness; he will do all tasks: will dig, will haul cannons, vehicles; he will man outposts, escort convoys; he will work on whatever he is ordered.

The spirit of seeking battle: The Legion, from the lone man to the entire Legion, will hasten always to where firing is heard, by day, by night, always, always, even though not ordered to do so.

The spirit of discipline: He will accomplish his duty, he will obey until death.

The spirit of combat: The Legion will demand always, always, to fight, out of turn, without counting the days, nor the months, nor the years.

The spirit of death: To die in combat is the greatest honour. One does not die more than once. Death comes without pain and to die is not as terrible as it appears. More terrible is to live as a coward.

The flag of the Legion: It will be the most glorious because it will be stained with the blood of its legionaries.

All legionaries are brave. Each nation has a reputation of courage. Here it is necessary to demonstrate which people is the most valiant.

In addition to this Credo, Millán Astray gave the Legion a battle-cry: *'Viva la Muerte!'*—Long live death! Soon the Legion would have its own hymns:

The 1st and 2nd Banderas parade before the High Commissioner, Gen. Berenguer, at Dar Drius on 7 March 1922, led by Comandante Franco (on left) and Lt.Col. José Millán Astray (right front). (Agencia Efe)

'*Song of the Legionary*', '*Hymn of the Legionaries*', '*The Betrothed of Death*', and always very popular—the Legion's version of the French marching-song, '*La Madelón*'. When in a suitable location the legionaries were allowed plenty of scope for wine, women and merriment, but during duty hours life was hard and discipline severe. Each bandera had a Punishment Squad in which defaulters performed long hours of back-breaking labour under the most rigorous supervision. Serious misdemeanours could mean a death sentence. And death—to whom their song declared they were betrothed—was certainly awaiting many of the legionaries in the precipitous mountains and stony deserts where they were soon to fight their battles.

Legionaries defending a sand-bagged outpost against a rebel attack. Note sergeant on the extreme left, wearing leather leggings and holding a '*fusta*' lash. (Agencia Efe)

The legionary standing third from right in the previous photograph has been hit by a Rifian bullet and is being evacuated by the legionary from the adjoining loophole (note Legion emblem on slouch hat), the sergeant and a medical orderly. (Agencia Efe)

Melilla: 1921-23

In the Western Zone (Ceuta) of the Spanish Protectorate a notorious rebel chieftain, El Raisuni, was once more instigating attacks against military posts and convoys. The High Commissioner of the Protectorate, Gen. Berenguer, sent against El Raisuni three columns of troops, which occupied the holy city of Xaüen by 14 October 1920 and then continued to advance along the Gomara coast. Though its training was not yet complete, the Legion was ordered into the field from its depôt at Dar Riffien.

On 3 November the 1st Bandera departed for Uad Lau, and on the 30th the 2nd and 3rd Banderas left for Zoco el Arbaa and Ben Karrich respectively. Much to the chagrin of Millán Astray and Franco, there followed several months during which the banderas were not permitted a place in the vanguard of any column and consequently experienced little action. However, on 27 June 1921, at two hill positions called 'Muñoz Crespo' and Buharrat, both the 1st and 3rd Banderas successfully fought off rebel bands, suffering 40 casualties between them.

A month later, on the night of 21 July, the 1st and 3rd Banderas and the 4th Company of the 2nd were camped on the slopes of Rokba Gozal, overlooking El Raisuni's stronghold at Tazarut, which was now effectively surrounded by Gen. Berenguer's forces. At 2 am on the 22nd, Millán Astray informed Franco that a bandera had to leave for Fondak immediately on an undisclosed mission. Consequently, at 4 am, Franco led the 1st Bandera and the 4th Company of the 2nd northwards.

After marching all day on a circuitous route under the burning African sun, the bandera reached Fondak as midnight approached. Lashed by a fierce gale, the legionaries fell into an exhausted sleep by the roadside, but by 3.30 am they were once more on the march, after Franco had received insistent telephoned instructions from Gen. Berenguer in Tetuán. Arriving at Tetuán by 9.45 am, the bandera completed a 60-mile forced march during which two legionaries had died from exhaustion. Here the 1st Bandera was united with the 2nd and, before both units were transported by train up the coast to Ceuta, they heard rumours of a disaster which had occurred in the Eastern Zone of the Protectorate.

Spanish forces, under the command of Gen. Silvestre, had been forced to retreat from a village called Annual, about ten miles to the south-east of Alhucemas. A charismatic and very able former official of the Bureau of Native Affairs in Melilla, Mohamed Abd el Krim of the Beni Urriaguel tribe, had rallied the *kabyles* of the Rif against Silvestre.

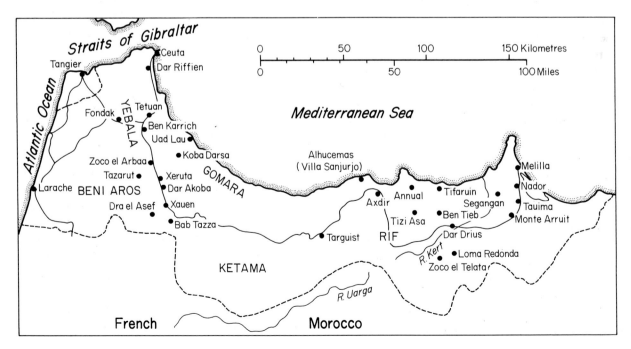

The retreating column was constantly assailed by the tribesmen, who wreaked a great slaughter, knifing the wounded to death and castrating the dead. By the night of 23 July the triumphant rebels had bypassed the shattered remnants of the column and swarmed on to the three crests of the Gurugú mountain, overlooking Melilla. Behind them more than 9,000 mutilated Spanish corpses littered the route from Annual.

At 6 pm that evening in Ceuta the 1st and 2nd Banderas, joined by Gen. Sanjurjo and Lt.Col. Millán Astray, boarded the ferry boat *Ciudad de Cádiz*. When the ferry docked in Melilla harbour at 2 pm on the 24th it was greeted by crowds of panic-stricken Spanish citizens. To boost their morale Millán Astray harangued the crowds on the quayside:

'People of Melilla! The Legion which comes to save you salutes you. We are prepared to die for you. We are under the orders of the heroic Gen. Sanjurjo, and we shall triumph. Away with fear! The breasts of the Legion stand between you and the enemy. Long live Spain! Long live Melilla! Long live the Legion!'

The 1st and 2nd Banderas now marched through the city streets with their standards unfurled and singing '*La Madelón*'. With their confidence restored, Melilla's citizens hailed the legionaries as their saviours. Gen. Sanjurjo then despatched the two banderas to man defensive positions in the suburbs. Two tabors of Regulares of Ceuta arrived the following day, as did three Spanish infantry battalions.

After the Legion and Regulares had advanced to and occupied the hills of Sidi Hamed and the Atalayón they were permitted to advance no further. During the following seven weeks the two banderas fought numerous actions while escorting convoys of pack-mules carrying water, rations and ammunition to forward positions, where small detachments of legionaries regularly fought off Rifian attacks upon their sandbagged blockhouses. On 8 September Millán Astray and Franco fought together in the vanguard of a column escorting a convoy to a strongpoint at Casabona. Supported by two tabors of Regulares of Ceuta, Franco led the 2nd Bandera and two companies of the 1st in a bayonet charge against a large enemy concentration in well-entrenched positions dominating

Franco with (on his right) Comandante José Puig García, commander of the 5th Bandera, following the capture of a Rifian strongpoint at Tizzi Asa on 28 October 1922. (Agencia Efe)

the route. In the determined Rifian counter-attacks which followed close-quarter fighting caused severe casualties. More than 90 legionaries were killed or wounded, and about 100 Regulares.

On 14 September a blockhouse at Dar Hamed, which was in an exposed position and was consequently known as 'El Malo'—the bad one—was relieved by troops from an army Disciplinary Battalion. On the afternoon of the 15th Rifian artillery fire gravely wounded the officer in charge, and the blockhouse was soon surrounded by the enemy and under siege. Lt. Agulla, in command of a detachment of the 1st Bandera on the Atalayón, assembled his men and asked for volunteers to reinforce 'El Malo', though it would mean certain death. All of his men volunteered. The lieutenant therefore selected from among them Cpl. Suceso Terrero and 14 legionaries, who then made their final requests. As darkness fell the 15 volunteers reached the blockhouse, sustaining two wounded

Lt.Col. Rafael de Valenzuela, accompanied by a Legion captain, on Spanish Red Cross flag day in May 1923, less than a month before he was killed in a bayonet charge at Tizzi Asa. Valenzuela wears the 'teresiana' cap. (Agencia Efe)

when a bullet struck the former in the chest and knocked him down. After exclaiming, 'They have killed me!' Millán Astray exposed the profusely bleeding wound above his heart, then jumped to his feet, shouting 'Long live Spain! Long live the King! Long live the Legion!' After Franco had helped him on to a stretcher, Millán Astray was evacuated to the Red Cross Hospital in Melilla, from where he would be sent home to Spain a few days later.

Franco now led the 1st and 2nd Banderas along the edge of the gorge under heavy fire, and drove the enemy from several heights as far as Monte Arbós. That day the two banderas sustained 33 casualties. On entering Nador the following day, the banderas were greeted by the stench of the savagely mutilated Spanish corpses that had littered the town for weeks. During the next six days the legionaries buried the dead in a large communal grave.

In October a 4th Bandera was formed at Dar Riffien. An extra rifle company was now authorised for each bandera. The companies were numbered as follows: *1st Bandera*—1, 2, 3 and 13; *2nd*—4, 5, 6 and 14; *3rd*—7, 8, 9 and 15; and *4th*—10, 11, 12 and 16; 3, 6, 9 and 12 were machine gun companies. The 13th and 14th Companies, which joined the 1st and 2nd Banderas in the field on 24 October, contained an influx of recruits from Central and South America. During this period there were some British legionaries in the 1st Company who—their company commander noted—became distressed when unable to make tea!

Berenguer's offensive was now directed west towards the River Kert, with the Legion, led by Franco, always in the vanguard of Sanjurjo's column. On 2 October the 1st and 2nd Banderas and the Regulares of Ceuta successfully assaulted ravines and trenches at Sebt, the Legion suffering 150 casualties. On the 5th Sanjurjo's column took Atlatlen; on the 8th, Segangan; and on the 10th, during heavy fighting on the crests of the Gurugú mountain, the two banderas sustained 121 casualties. When Monte Arruit was occupied on the 24th the legionaries had to bury at least 800 putrefying corpses of troops who had tried to make a stand there during the retreat from Annual.

In November the weather grew cold and there was torrential rain and sleet. The territory of the *kabyle* of Beni bu Ifrur was dominated by forts on a

before they could cross the barbed wire. Inside, they found several soldiers dead. The Rifians now attacked with even greater vigour, but the legionaries held them at bay with grenades and rifle fire. Towards midnight the tribesmen brought up their artillery and pounded the blockhouse at close range. In a matter of minutes 'El Malo' was reduced to rubble, with the defenders buried beneath it.

By mid-September Gen. Berenguer felt he had assembled sufficient troops in Melilla to give Gen. Sanjurjo orders to lead a column against Nador, ten miles to the south. At 7 am on the 17th, as warships, floating batteries, artillery and an air squadron all commenced a bombardment of Rifian positions, the 1st and 2nd Banderas, the Regulares of Ceuta and three Spanish infantry battalions advanced from Sidi Hamed under Rifian artillery fire from the Gurugú mountain. At the Amadi gorge the vanguard was halted by concentrated enemy machine gun and rifle fire. Millán Astray and Franco were conferring at the most forward point massive mountain called Uisán. In the early hours of 18 November, after silently scaling the steep slope of a ravine carrying their machine guns and munitions, the two banderas and indigenous police seized the old forts on the heights. During the following days, as the cold grew more intense, operations were extended to Ras Medua, Tauriat Hamed and El Harcha.

Meanwhile, in the Western Zone (Ceuta), the new 4th Bandera, on 23 and 28 October, suffered total casualties of 72 dead and 212 wounded in bayonet charges against rebel 'harcas' (bands) surrounding Monte Magán. A 5th Bandera was formed at Dar Riffien in November and would also soon be in action. Lt.Col. Millán Astray arrived back in Ceuta on 10 November, still not fully recovered from his chest wound. Nonetheless he put himself at the head of the 3rd, 4th and 5th Banderas, operating with columns in the Beni Arós and Yebala regions. Then, on 10 January 1922, during a withdrawal from a position at Dráa el Asef—in which the 8th Company fought with knives when

assailed by an enemy force ten times their number—Millán Astray was wounded by a bullet in the right leg. Due to this and his still unhealed chest wound, he was once more evacuated to Spain on 18 January.

During the following months the 3rd, 4th and 5th Banderas continued to man positions and protect convoys principally around Xaüen; and on 12 May the 3rd and 5th participated in the final occupation of Tazarut—from where El Raisuni had fled into hiding.

In the Eastern Zone (Melilla), Dar Drius was captured on 10 January 1922. Millán Astray, once more recovered, arrived at the Legion's camp there on 14 February. Gen. Berenguer resumed operations in mid-March, leading a column against the Beni Said and Beni Ulixech. Consequently, on 18 March, Millán Astray led the 1st and 2nd Banderas

Lt. Col. Franco (first on left) in his field command post in the Dar Drius sector in mid-1923, beside Capt. González Badía, observing the artillery preparation before ordering an attack. (Agencia Efe)

Legionaries open fire, covering an advance into rebel-held territory. A two-man team operates a 7 mm Hotchkiss machine gun, backed by a rifle squad. (Agencia Efe)

in an advance on Ambar. After repulsing fierce enemy counter-attacks the Legion had sustained 86 casualties, including Comandante Fontanes, commander of the 2nd Bandera, who was fatally wounded in the stomach.

A 6th Bandera was formed in September at Dar Riffien; and in November the 2nd Bandera commenced the construction of a large advanced camp for the Legion at Ben Tieb. Due to internal rivalries within the Spanish military establishment (basically between Spain-based officers and 'Africanistas'), a Royal Order of 13 November disposed that Millán Astray be transferred from command of the Legion to a regiment in the province of Cádiz. Appointed in his place was 41-year-old Lt.Col. Rafael de Valenzuela Urzais, who had founded and conspicuously commanded the Group of Regulares of Alhucemas. Franco now requested, and received, a posting back to his old regiment in Oviedo, departing from the Legion on 17 January 1923.

Valenzuela's command was to be short-lived.

On 5 June 1923 a column commanded by Col. Gómez Morato started out from Tafersit to escort a convoy of food and ammunition to the beleaguered outpost of Tizzi Asa. In the vanguard were the 1st, 2nd and 4th Banderas, under the Legion's new commander, and a tabor of Regulares. The Regulares were held up in the Iguermisen ravine by the fire of a large and well-entrenched rebel *harca*. On the right flank the 1st and 2nd Banderas tried to fight their way through to the ravine, and the 4th pushed forward on the left flank. While the Legion's machine guns swept the Rifian positions, Col. Gómez Morato, placed on the extreme right of the deployment, ordered a general attack. Lt.Col. Valenzuela now exclaimed to the men of the 2nd Bandera, 'Legionaries, the moment has come to die for Spain!' and his bugler sounded the Legion's call *'Legionaries to fight, legionaries to die'* and the attack. The 2nd Bandera then charged with fixed bayonets up the slope towards the Rifian entrenchments. Valenzuela followed with his escort, and the 1st Bandera also charged. In a mêlée of individual combats the legionaries drove the rebels from their trenches with grenades and bayonets. Valenzuela, shouting encouragement and firing his pistol, was hit by a bullet in the head and another in the chest. The members of his escort were shot down around him, as were four pairs of stretcher-bearers sent to collect his body. Scattered groups of legionaries now rallied behind the nearest officer in a final charge which drove the Rifians into retreat. Legion casualties totalled 186.

On 8 June Franco was promoted to lieutenant-colonel and given command of the Legion. Once more he postponed his intended wedding and took the ferry boat to Morocco. Between 22 June and 16 July Franco travelled from location to location in both zones, inspecting and fighting with his six banderas. The besieged outpost of Tifaruin, near the mouth of the River Kert, was encircled by 9,000 Rifian tribesmen. On 22 August Regulares of Alhucemas and Melilla, trying to break through, met with stiff resistance. After leading the 1st and 2nd Banderas in a wide right envelopment Franco attacked the enemy entrenchments from the flank and rear, and thus permitted the Regulares to advance through to relieve Tifaruin.

Between 12 and 15 September 1923 a *coup d'état* was enacted in Spain. In a climate of numerous political assassinations and rapidly deteriorating public order, Gen. Miguel Primo de Rivera, Captain-General of Catalonia, took over the reins of government. Franco arrived in Madrid on 16 October on 40 days' leave. He advocated to King Alfonso, and later to Primo de Rivera, a plan to finally defeat the Rifian rebels by landing from the sea on the beaches of Alhucemas Bay and then capturing Abd el Krim's headquarters at Axdir. Then, in Oviedo on 22 October, Lt.Col. Francisco Franco at last married Carmen Polo Martínez-Valdés. Among many congratulatory telegrams from Legion posts was one from eight imprisoned legionaries in Ceuta, who stressed that their crime was not desertion.

A section of legionaries in action, parapeted behind the crumbling walls of a destroyed building. Note the bugler, third from right. (Agencia Efe)

Xaüen and Alhucemas: 1924-27

As 1924 began the 1st, 2nd, 3rd and 4th Banderas were all concentrated in the advanced camp of Ben Tieb. Franco arrived here on 25 February and, during the next four months, personally led his banderas in numerous hard-fought operations to allow passage of convoys to Tizzi Asa, Sidi Mesaud and other outposts. By June the *kabyles* of Beni Said, Beni Hassan, Beni Hosmar and many others in the Western Zone had recognised the leadership of Abd el Krim, self-proclaimed Emir of the Rif. His consequently large army of approximately 80,000 warriors was well supplied with captured and purchased armaments, including some 200 artillery pieces.

The most threatened sectors in the Western Zone were the valley of the Lau, the Tetuán-Xaüen road and the gorges of Beni Arós. By mid-August Primo de Rivera had decided to withdraw from all three, falling back to the more defendable coastal fringes and protecting the city of Tetuán and its lines of communication with Larache, Tangier and Ceuta. Troops would be withdrawn to the new line from more than 400 forward positions. In August the 1st, 5th and 6th Banderas were all deployed in the Western Zone, and on the 31st of that month the 2nd, 3rd and 4th embarked at Melilla, destination Ceuta.

Withdrawal from the Lau sector had begun on 20 August 1924. Abd el Krim immediately stepped up his attacks in the area. As a result Primo de Rivera and several members of his Directorate left Madrid for Tetuán on 5 September, at a time when Tetuán itself was under threat. The *harcas* of Abd el Krim controlled the Gorgues mountains to the south-east of the city. The 2nd, 3rd, 4th and 5th Banderas all operated with columns, clearing the enemy from these commanding heights during the first three weeks of September. This both thwarted Abd el Krim's designs on Tetuán and was a first stage towards opening the road to Xaüen. Ten thousand Spanish soldiers stationed in the holy city and numerous posts around it were now surrounded and in danger of annihilation. This included the 6th Bandera.

To evacuate these forces, two columns left Tetuán on 23 September 1924, commanded by Gen. Castro Girona and Gen. Serrano, with the 1st, 3rd, 4th and 5th Banderas placed in the vanguards. Despite fierce enemy opposition on the route, Serrano's column entered Xaüen on 30 September and Castro Girona's on 2 October. During the next seven weeks detachments of legionaries and Regulares were sent out to evacuate more than 100 forward outposts and concentrate all military personnel in Xaüen, incurring many losses in the process.

On 16 October, in Tetuán, Gen. Primo de Rivera appointed himself High Commissioner and General Officer Commanding in the Spanish Protectorate. By the 30th of that month his plan to evacuate the Beni Arós sector had been successfully accomplished. The 2nd Bandera had performed brilliantly in protecting the withdrawal. Evacuation from the remaining positions in Gomara was at the same time well advanced. There only remained Xaüen.

A happy Col. Franco (right), accompanied by Lt.Col. González Badía, approaches his command post on the just-captured Monte Malmusi on 23 September 1925, after the consolidation of the Alhucemas bridgehead. (Agencia Efe)

In the early hours of 15 November all Spanish troops and civilians, plus many Moroccan and Jewish citizens, left Xaüen on the road to Tetuán, again in two columns with Generals Serrano and Castro Girona commanding. Numerous *harcas* and organised units of the Beni Urriaguel lost no time in making flanking attacks upon the Spanish columns. To the rear, the five banderas of the Legion held Xaüen until, in the first hour of the 17th, Franco led them silently out of the city. Left manning the parapets were hundreds of straw dummies clad in the green tunics and caps of the Legion, which Franco had given the order to prepare in secret a week before. It was several hours before the deception was discovered by the enemy.

Franco's Legion rearguard reached Dar Akoba and, over the following two days, lashed by heavy rain and gales, continued to protect the withdrawal and evacuate posts by way of Xeruta and Hamra to Zoco el Arbaa. Capt. Arredondo's 1st Company was completely wiped out while covering the withdrawal from Xeruta. After Gen. Serrano was killed there was only one column, and it remained totally surrounded at Zoco el Arbaa for three weeks. Breaking out on 10 December, the column proceeded by Taranes and Zinat, with the Legion rearguard again involved in hard fighting, often hand-to-hand. Then, early on the 13th, the five banderas followed the remnants of the bedraggled, exhausted column into Ben Karrich in the approaches to Tetuán. The number of Spanish lives lost in the evacuation from Xaüen is unlikely to have exceeded 2,000. Total Legion casualties (dead and wounded) for the whole operation were about 1,000.

Primo de Rivera had now achieved his objective, with his forces grouped along and behind a line of defendable positions. He was extremely pleased with Franco, and approved his promotion to full colonel, made official on 7 February 1925. On 16 February a Royal Order changed the Legion's title from 'Tercio of Foreigners' to 'Tercio of Morocco'. A 7th Bandera was formed at Dar Riffien on 1 May, as was a mounted Squadron of Lancers; and the following day yet another Royal Order countermanded that of 16 February and reduced the Legion's official title simply to 'Tercio'.

The Tercio was now organised in two Legions, as follows: *Eastern Zone (Melilla)*: 1st Legion—1st,

Col. Millán Astray, minus his left arm, jokes while pointing out an enemy position to a junior Legion officer in February 1926. (Agencia Efe)

2nd, 3rd and 4th Banderas. *Western Zone (Ceuta)*: 2nd Legion—5th, 6th and 7th Banderas (to be joined later by the 8th, raised 1 January 1926). The Squadron of Lancers was directly under the orders of the colonel commanding the Tercio, and performed escort and reconnaissance duties. (Serving personnel, from the colonel to the newest recruit, nevertheless continued to call the Tercio 'the Legion' and referred to the two Legions as 'Tercios'!)

On 9 April 1925 Abd el Krim launched five *harcas* of his army against French positions along the Uarga River. By June, 43 out of 66 forward posts had fallen and more than 3,000 French troops were dead or missing. Nearly all of the local *kabyles* rallied to Abd el Krim, who was now within striking distance of Taza and Fez and was a feasible threat to Rabat and Casablanca. Marshal Pétain, the hero of Verdun during the 1914–18 War, was summoned from France to command hurriedly reinforced French troops in Morocco.

After a month of French–Spanish discussions in Madrid, Pétain and Primo de Rivera met together in Tetuán on 28 July to finalise plans for a combined offensive against their common foe. It was agreed that 160,000 French troops would attack Abd el Krim from the south, while 18,000

Spanish landed at Alhucemas Bay, and another 57,000 pressed an attack from Spain's Eastern Zone.

The Alhucemas landings

Pétain launched his offensive along the Uarga River on 28 August. Aware of the Spanish intentions, Abd el Krim tried to create a diversion by posing a threat to Tetuán and, on 3 September, mounted a siege of the fort at Cudia Tahar in the Gorgues mountains. Undeterred, Primo de Rivera, exercising personal overall command, gave Gen. Sanjurjo direct command of two columns, each 9,000 strong, to land at Alhucemas: the Ceuta Column under Gen. Saro and the Melilla Column under Gen. Fernández Pérez. The Ceuta Column was scheduled to land first, and on 7 September its transport ships, escorted by warships of the Spanish navy, stood off a beach called La Cebadilla, actually to the north-west of Alhucemas Bay.

At 6.30 am on 8 September 1925, 32 Spanish and 18 French naval vessels, to the north and east of the landing areas, commenced their bombardment, aiming principally at the 20 well-installed Rifian batteries on the crests overlooking the beaches. This was followed up, two hours later, by bombing and strafing by 76 aircraft. During this time the transports, which had been scattered westward during the night by the strong current, were brought back into position. Towards 11 am tugs and gunboats began to tow the lines of K21 and K23 landing craft (types used by the British at Gallipoli) towards La Cebadilla and the adjoining Ixdain beaches. In the first line Col. Franco commanded ten light tanks, the 6th and 7th Banderas, the Mehal-la (native police) of Larache, a Rifian *harca* of irregular levies (commanded by Soliman el Jatabi—Abd el Krim's cousin!), the Spanish Battalion of Africa No. 3, and a mountain battery.

Rifian artillery began to shell the approaching tugs and gunboats. A thousand yards from the shore the landing craft cast off and continued alone under their own power. Machine gun and rifle fire raked the craft as they ran aground on shoals 50 yards from the shore. The ramps were quickly lowered, but efforts to unload the tanks proved futile. Franco gave the order to attack, and his bugler sounded the call.

The legionaries and Moroccans leapt into the water, holding their rifles over their heads. First on to the beach were men of the 24th Company, 6th Bandera. The 22nd Company landed further east, and the Machine Gun Company established a fire base to cover the advance. Also soon ashore were Franco and the 7th Bandera. Franco ordered the assault of the dominating crests—the two banderas attacking on the left, the *harca* on the right and the Mehal-la in the centre. As the legionaries scaled the heights of El Fraile and Morro Nuevo, bayoneted Rifian corpses began to hurtle down to the beach below. By 3 pm the crests, with an artillery battery on each, had been captured and—as Franco later wrote—'those who resisted too much were put to the knife'. All units now dug in along the crests, still under heavy Rifian bombardment. The Spanish had suffered 124 total casualties in the landing; more than 8,000 troops and three batteries had been brought ashore, and the tanks had eventually been landed on the beach of Los Frailes.

Meanwhile, at the besieged fort of Cudia Tahar near Tetuán, 176 of the 200 men of the garrison had been killed by 8 September. Primo de Rivera therefore ordered the 2nd and 3rd Banderas, with the Melilla Column, to abandon their imminent landing at Alhucemas and proceed to Ceuta. After arrival there on the 10th the banderas continued to Tetuán, where they joined Gen. Sousa's relief column. After fierce hand-to-hand fighting in an assault on the village of Dar Gazi the two banderas spearheaded the relief of Cudia Tahar on the 13th, having suffered 144 casualties in the operation. The banderas then returned to Alhucemas and, on the 19th, rejoined the Melilla Column which had landed on the beach of Los Frailes eight days earlier.

In the face of repeated Rifian counter-attacks against the bridgehead, 15,000 Spanish troops had disembarked by 20 September 1925. Rough seas had meanwhile provoked a temporary supply crisis, but by the 22nd sufficient food, ammunition and pack-mules had arrived to enable the Spanish to strike out from their bridgehead. Preceded by air and artillery bombardment, at 6.20 am on the 23rd, Comandante Muñoz Grandes (later to command the 'Blue Division' in Russia, 1941[1]) led the Rifian *harca* forward on the left flank, followed by the 6th

[1]See MAA 103, *Germany's Spanish Volunteers 1941–45*

and 7th Banderas. After crossing minefields, the attack swept over a preliminary enemy line of defence. Then, at 10.45 am, the three units launched the final assault on the heights of Monte Malmusi under sustained fire from artillery and Rifians concentrated in lines of trenches. The legionaries cleared the enemy from their trenches and also from numerous caves, principally using mortars, grenades, bayonets and knives. By early morning they had killed all who still resisted and had themselves sustained 215 casualties. On that same day the 2nd and 3rd Banderas, with the Melilla Column to the east, had assaulted and seized the heights of Morro Viejo and lower Malmusi.

On 30 September the Ceuta Column took Monte Palomas against stiff resistance, while the Melilla Column captured the heights of Cónico and Buyibar. The Rifians were by now in retreat everywhere. The French, attacking along the Uarga, had expelled all enemy forces from their territory and were continuing to advance. Spanish troops entered Abd el Krim's capital of Axdir on 2 October, and set fire to it. On the 8th French and Spanish forces linked up at Zoco el Telata.

On 3 February 1926 Franco was promoted to brigadier-general and, at the age of 33, had become the youngest general both in Spain and in Europe. A Royal Order of 9 February consequently returned command of the Legion to Millán Astray, who had been promoted to full colonel on 21 October 1924 while on the staff of the High Commissioner. Just five days after this promotion, on proceeding to Fondak to take command of a Spanish column, he had become involved in an action in which his left arm was shattered by a bullet and later, growing gangrenous, had to be amputated. On 10 February 1926 the one-armed warrior happily arrived in Ceuta to take command of the Legion from his old comrade-in-arms, and on the 17th Franco left for Madrid.

Some 140,000 Spanish and 325,000 French troops now prepared to launch a spring offensive from their consolidated lines of the Axdir bridgehead, the Uarga and the upper Kert against the 40 *kabyles* that still remained under arms in Yebala, Gomara and the Rif. On the morning of 4 March 1926 the 8th Bandera captured a hill called Loma Redonda in the Gorgues mountains. After ordering the hilltop to be fortified with posts for six machine

guns and four mortars, Millán Astray later returned to inspect the work despite continuous fire from enemy positions on Hafa el Duira. At 3.30 pm, as he approached the first post, he was struck in the face by a bullet which destroyed his right eye, lacerated his jaw and came out through his left cheek. Characteristically, he still managed to shout 'Viva España! Viva la Legión!' before being evacuated in a very grave condition.

On 15 April the French began their new offensive from the River Uarga while, from 8 May, the Spanish advanced south against the 12,000 tribesmen, principally Beni Urriaguel, who were

Col. Millán Astray, now minus both his left arm and right eye, addresses assembled forces at Alhucemas late in 1926. Note bullet-exit scar on his left cheek, and four wound chevrons on his left sleeve. (Agencia Efe)

17

still resisting in the central Rif. For three days, 8–10 May, the 1st, 2nd, 4th, 5th, 7th and 8th Banderas, with forces of Regulares, Mehal-la and Spanish infantry, fought on and around the heights of Loma de los Morabos south-east of Axdir, inflicting further defeat on the Beni Urriaguel, whose remnants fell back everywhere before the inland drives of the Spanish and French forces. Their leader, Abd el Krim, finally surrendered to French troops at Targuist on 27 May 1926, and was exiled in September to Réunion Island in the Indian Ocean.

On 28 July, after treatment in Madrid, Millán Astray was once more at Dar Riffien with his legionaries, with a black patch covering the empty socket of his right eye and the left sleeve of his tunic equally vacant. During the last six months of 1926 the eight banderas moved from location to location, always in the vanguard of columns, protecting convoys and pacifying and disarming the *kabyles*. In the heart of the Rif, bordering the French zone, the *kabyle* of Ketama and associated smaller tribal groups rose in rebellion early in 1927. The 1st, 2nd, 3rd, 6th and 8th Banderas, operating principally from Targuist, took the field in the snow and ice of March. After long marches over mountainous terrain and numerous clashes with the enemy, the Spanish columns pacified the territory by June.

A Royal Order of 18 June 1927 promoted Millán Astray to brigadier-general and thus finally ended his command of the Legion, with whom he had personally fought in 62 actions. The following month, on 10 July, when Spanish forces including the 7th Bandera occupied Bab Tazza in Gomara, the entire Spanish Protectorate was officially declared pacified. In 845 battles the Legion had sustained casualties of 2,000 dead, 6,096 wounded and 285 missing. Collective awards of the Military Medal were made to the 1st, 2nd and 4th Banderas. There were 12 individual awards of the Laureate Cross of St Ferdinand and 49 Individual Military Medals awarded. In a final tribute, a Royal Order of 1 October named Gen. Millán Astray as Honorary Colonel of the Tercio.

Field Mass at Dar Riffien on 5 October 1927 as part of the ceremony in which Queen Victoria Eugenia presented the Legion with its first national standard (see Plates B1 and B2). Left to right: the Bishop of Gallipoli (resident in Tangier), Col. Sanz de Larín; a junior officer with the flag; and the much-decorated and much-wounded Capt. Lizcano de la Rosa, who wears Spain's highest gallantry award, the Laureate Cross of St Ferdinand. (Agencia Efe)

18

Asturias and the National Rising: 1934-36

On 14 April 1931, more than a year after the end of Primo de Rivera's dictatorship, King Alfonso XIII went into voluntary exile and the Second Spanish Republic was proclaimed. Subsequent reductions in the military establishment included the disbandment of the 7th and 8th Banderas and the Squadron of Lancers on 27 December 1932.

As a consequence of election results in November 1933 which predominantly favoured right-wing candidates, an armed revolution was launched on 5 October 1934 in the mining valleys of the northern province of Asturias, accompanied by a general strike and disturbances in Madrid and Catalonia. Under the direction of a Revolutionary Committee of Socialists, Communists and Anarcho-Sindicalists, 30,000 miners, well supplied with small arms, dynamite, 200 machine guns and 29 artillery pieces seized from the arms factory of Trubia, attacked and captured several Asturian towns including the capital, Oviedo. The Minister of War, Diego Hidalgo, advised by Gen. Franco, despatched columns of troops to Asturias from neighbouring provinces and summoned reinforcements from the Moroccan Protectorate.

The 3rd, 5th and 6th Banderas were all shipped to Spain and were soon in action against the revolutionaries. Lt.Col. Juan Yagüe Blanco, who had served in Morocco with the Regulares of Melilla, Tetuán, Larache and Ceuta, was given command of a column consisting of the 5th and 6th Banderas, a tabor of Regulares of Ceuta and a battalion of Light Infantry of Africa. After liberating Gijón and Lugones the column reached Oviedo on 12 October. Supported by other government units, Yagüe's column had to fight for three days, house by house and district by district, against fanatical resistance, before they took the town. After negotiations on the 18th the Asturian rebels agreed to capitulate, and the following day five government columns marched into the mining valleys. Yagüe's column occupied the revolutionaries' stronghold at Mieres.

Five Individual Military Medals were awarded to the Legion during this short campaign. Legion casualties were only 13 dead and 46 wounded, but the short-lived Red revolution had cost Spain 1,335 lives and enormous material damage to churches, factories and public buildings.

On 16 February 1936 a new left-wing government—the Popular Front—was elected to office by a narrow margin of votes. In a rapidly deteriorating situation of strikes, riots, church-burnings and assassinations which left 330 people dead and 1,511 injured in five months, Spanish political groups of both left and right prepared for the inevitable final clash. After the murder of the Monarchist opposition leader José Calvo Sotelo by pro-government Assault Guards in the early hours of 13 July, Spain was irrevocably divided.

In July 1936 the Tercio was stationed in the Spanish Protectorate of Morocco as follows: *Eastern Zone (Melilla)*: 1st Legion—1st, 2nd and 3rd Banderas, based at Tauima, Targuist and Villa Sanjurjo; *Western Zone (Ceuta)*: 2nd Legion—4th, 5th and 6th Banderas, based at Dar Riffien, Zoco el Arbaa and Xaüen. Lt.Col. Yagüe had been appointed commander of the 2nd Legion at Dar Riffien on 28 January, and since then had been clandestinely organising a rising in Morocco as a preliminary to an intended 'National Rising' in Spain. The hour eventually agreed between Gen. Emilio Mola (Military Governor of Pamplona, and 'director' of the conspiracy) and Yagüe for action in the Protectorate was 1700 hrs on 17 July.

On the afternoon of the 17th, however, investigations by Republican police in Melilla precipitated the conspirators' action. The 1st and 2nd Banderas, supported by the Group of Regulares of Melilla, seized control of Melilla after sporadic skirmishes with armed Marxist militiamen. That night the 5th Bandera marched on Tetuán, where there was, in fact, little local resistance. By the morning of the 18th Ceuta and Larache had fallen easily into the insurgents' hands, and the entire Moroccan Protectorate could be declared secured for the National Rising, which was now erupting in Spain itself.

Allocated by Gen. Mola the task of taking command of the Army of Africa, Gen. Franco arrived in Tetuán on the morning of the 19th, having flown from Las Palmas, Canary Islands. At that same time, in Spain, thousands of red-bereted Traditionalist volunteers were descending from their villages in the mountains of Navarre to rally behind Gen. Mola in Pamplona, while blue-shirted Falangists joined the military in the streets of Zaragoza, Burgos and Valladolid. It was Mola's plan that columns from these cities would thrust towards Madrid from the north while the Army of Africa would march on the capital from the south.

Airlift from Africa

In Tetuán, Franco immediately applied himself to the task of transporting the Army of Africa to the Spanish mainland. Most of the fleet was under the control of the Republican government (as was more than half the army and two-thirds of the air force), making sea crossings extremely hazardous. So Franco decreed that seven Breguet I aircraft in Tetuán's aerodrome would be used to transport the 5th Bandera to the aid of the sparse and hard-pressed forces of Gen. Queipo de Llano in Seville, each aircraft carrying 16 men and making four flights daily. Two platoons of the 17th Company were the first legionaries to cross the Straits by air, arriving safely in Seville on 20 July. In the days that followed the remainder of the 5th Bandera was

Lt.Col. Juan Yagüe arrives in Seville on 6 August 1936 to take command of the 'Madrid Column'. (Agencia Efe)

flown in and completed the occupation of Seville.

Over a period of four weeks all of the Legion's banderas were transported to Spain. On 5 August the entire 1st Bandera, accompanied by two tabors of Regulares, a battery of artillery and 50 tons of ammunition, made the crossing by sea from Tetuán to Algeciras in a small convoy which, despite being attacked by a Republican destroyer, reached its destination safely. As additional aircraft became available from Italy and Germany the remaining banderas crossed by air—the 4th to Seville at the end of July, and the 6th, 2nd and 3rd to Jerez de la Frontera, Granada and Seville during the first three weeks in August. (By November 1936, 23,393 men of the Army of Africa had been flown across the Straits in this first 'air bridge' in military history.)

Civil War in Spain: 1936-39

Between 18 and 20 July 1936 the National Rising triumphed principally in the provinces of Galicia, Old Castile, León, Navarre, Alava and Aragón, which became known as the Nationalist Zone. With religion suppressed, churches destroyed and priests, monks and nuns murdered in their thousands in Republican Spain, the Spanish Church and many devout people of the Nationalist provinces—particularly Navarre—regarded the Spanish Civil War as a holy crusade. For others the war was a patriotic crusade to save their nation from destruction by anarchy and regional separatism, and from the threat of Communist tyranny. For many it was both. As their memorials proclaimed, they believed that they fought and died 'For God and for Spain'.

To dismiss the Spanish Nationalists as 'Fascists' on the grounds that they were supported by Nazi Germany and Fascist Italy is too simplistic a judgement, and is to rely upon hindsight. Hitler's use of the Spanish war to battle-test his aircraft and tanks was one price extracted for supplying the Nationalists with badly needed German armaments. As a condition for equivalent aid, the Republic's manipulation by Stalinist Russia was no less cynical, as perceptive foreign Republican volunteers such as George Orwell had the courage to point out. The Spanish people of those years chose sides according to their perceptions of purely local issues, in the light of their own ideals and loyalties: and to many Nationalists, their cause was genuinely a crusade.

To fight in this crusade 60,000 volunteers rallied to form 50 Traditionalist and Falangist militia battalions during the first three months of conflict, while more than half the strength of another 50 newly raised regular battalions were also volunteers. By September 1938 nearly a third of Franco's 500,000 infantry were volunteers. In the closing month of the war there were more than a million men in the Nationalist army, and all but 67,000 were Spanish. Women also made a substantial contribution to the cause—600,000 served in the Falange Feminine Section, 300,000 in Social Aid, 500,000 in the Traditionalist 'Margaritas' and 8,000 as army nurses.

On 1 August 1936 Gen. Franco issued an operational order for forces now concentrated in Seville to commence the march on Madrid. Two groups were instructed to proceed north by the main highway through Extremadura, secure the Portuguese frontier and make contact with Gen. Mola's forces in the north, then continue north-east to the capital. The two groups were commanded by Lt.Col. Asensio and Comandante Castejón and, accompanied by artillery and other supporting units, were principally composed as follows: *Group Asensio*—4th Bandera and 2nd Tabor of Regulares of Tetuán; *Group Castejón*—5th Bandera and 2nd Tabor of Regulares of Ceuta.

At 8 pm on 2 August Group Asensio set out from Seville, followed late the next day by Group Castejón. Borne in some 200 trucks and coaches, the 'Madrid Column' advanced 105 miles in five days, under regular attack from Republican aircraft and overcoming usually sporadic, but occasionally tough resistance from Republican militiamen in the small towns and villages along the route. Meanwhile, a third group was formed and sent north to join the march under the command of Lt.Col. Tella, mainly comprising the 1st Bandera of the Legion and the 1st Tabor of Regulares of Tetuán.

Badajoz
After the 'Madrid Column' had captured Mérida on 11 August, Lt. Col. Yagüe arrived from Seville to

The 1st Bandera is given an enthusiastic ovation by the people of Seville as it departs, on 10 August 1936, to join the march on Madrid. (Illustrated London News)

take direct command, with the immediate mission of securing the Spanish-Portuguese frontier. Leaving the 1st Bandera to defend Mérida against imminent counter-attack, Yagüe advanced westwards with his force of barely 3,000 men at dawn on the 12th. His objective was the town of Badajoz, which was protected by an encircling solid stone wall 60 feet in height. This wall and other strong points were defended by more than 5,000 well-armed Republican troops, both regular and milita. Legion officers who knew their history must have thoughtfully recalled that storming this same town in April 1812 had cost Wellington some 3,750 casualties.

The following day, at 3 pm, Yagüe launched his first attack. Under artillery cover, Group Asensio advanced into the district of San Roque which lay to the east outside the boundary wall, while Group Castejón stormed the Menacho barracks on the west side. That night Yagüe addressed his officers: 'Gentlemen of the Legion! The Reds affirm that you

are not soldiers but monks in disguise. Very well— enter Badajoz and say Mass!'

At dawn on the 14th the attack was resumed. On the east side the 2nd Tabor of Tetuán circled northwards by 11 am and fought its way into the town through a gate called Los Carros. An hour later, to the south, Lt. De Miguel led the 18th Company of the 5th Bandera across the bullet-swept esplanade of La Bomba barracks in a wild bayonet charge which completely demoralised the barracks' defenders. In the outlying eastern district of San Roque the 4th Bandera, under continuous mortar and machine gun fire, clung to its positions close to a gap in the wall by the Trinity Gate. This gap was 11 yards in length, and would forever be remembered in Legion history as 'la brecha de la muerte'—the breach of death.

At 3 pm Captain Pérez Caballero ordered the 16th Company to fix bayonets. His bugler then sounded the attack and, with an armoured car leading the way, the company charged the breach singing the Legion hymn 'The Betrothed of Death'. Republican machine gun fire cut down the leading platoon. Under a hail of grenades, Capt. Fuentes turned his armoured car to the right, drawing the

An unusually bulky captain, apparently unarmed, leading men of the 4th Bandera on the road to Badajoz in August 1936. Note the long cylindrical pouches for Lafitte grenades worn by the second man in the left file. (The Times)

enemy's fire. This enabled the second and third platoons to cross the dried-up bed of the River Rivillas and bombard the breach with hand grenades, creating a curtain of smoke which helped their further advance. Again, however, heavy automatic crossfire decimated the legionaries, who fell in scores, forming a heaped parapet of corpses and wounded from behind which two machine guns of the 12th Company were able to bring an effective fire to bear upon the sandbagged enemy machine gun emplacements.

Capt. Pérez Caballero now led the survivors of his company forward through concentrated machine gun and rifle fire across the bodies of nearly 80 fallen comrades. Legionary Rodríguez was cut down by automatic fire, holding the company flag aloft and yelling '*Viva la muerte!*' Beside him in the breach died Legionary Lluch, Legionary Martín and many more. The remnants fought their way through the breach and across the enemy parapets, hurling grenades and wielding bayonets and knives with uncontainable fury. The Republicans rapidly fell back up the narrow streets, pursued by the survivors of the 16th Company—Capt. Pérez Caballero, a corporal and 14 legionaries. On reaching the Town Hall the captain transmitted the following report to Yagüe: 'Have crossed the breach. I have 14 men. I do not need reinforcements!'

The 10th and 11th Companies nevertheless followed through the breach and advanced into the town, as did the other Nationalist units. Advancing street by street against stubborn resistance, the legionaries and Regulares gave no quarter. When the cease-fire came, Badajoz was littered with 1,000 corpses. Yagüe's forces had suffered a total of 285 casualties; of these, 106 belonged to the 4th Bandera.

Toledo and Madrid

During August and September 1936 the 2nd Bandera participated in the operations of Gen. Mola's forces in Guipúzcoa in which Irún, on the French frontier, was captured on 5 September. In October the 2nd Bandera was transferred to the Aragón front and the 3rd was diverted to operations in Asturias.

On 14 September Yagüe was promoted to Colonel Inspector (supreme commander) of the

Gen. Millán Astray, Honorary Colonel of the Legion, in uncharacteristic attire—wearing braces, and without insignia on his cap—attends a Nationalist rally in Zaragoza in September 1936. Immediately following him is a Legion officer. (Illustrated London News)

Legion. A week later, suffering from cardiac exhaustion, he was obliged temporarily to relinquish command of the 'Madrid Column', being replaced on the 24th by Gen. Varela. From Mérida the column had advanced north-east, capturing Talavera de la Reina on the 3rd and Maqueda on the 21st; but it was now diverted south-east to Toledo with instructions from Franco to proceed with all haste to the relief of a besieged fortress called the Alcázar. The heroic garrison (principally Civil Guards) and their families had withstood ten weeks of shells, bombs, mines, infantry assaults, hunger and thirst to hold the fortress for the Nationalist cause. On 27 September the 1st Tabor of Tetuán and the 5th Bandera were the first relief troops to embrace the emaciated but undefeated survivors in the rubble of the Alcázar.

On 1 October 1936 Gen. Franco was appointed Supreme Commander of the Armed Forces and Head of the Spanish State by the Provisional

Nationalist Junta. On the 6th, Gen. Varela continued his march on Madrid with four columns. Capturing Illescas on the 17th, Navalcarnero on the 21st and Valdemoro on the 31st, Varela's forces came within sight of the capital by 3 November. Though considerably reinforced, his columns—now including the 1st, 4th, 5th, 6th, 7th and 8th Banderas (the last two raised in September)—totalled no more than 15,000 men. Ready to oppose their entry into the city were 25,000 men of the Republican People's Army, then under formation from regular and Marxist militia units and the Communist International Brigades, which also (at that time) had superiority in tanks, artillery and air cover.

Two of Varela's columns managed to penetrate the Madrid suburbs of Carabanchel and Usera on 7 November, but from that day attack after attack made little progress. In the wooded parkland of the Casa del Campo and on the banks of the River Manzanares advancing legionaries and Regulares were decimated by artillery, mortar and machine gun fire. On the 15th Lt.Col. Asensio's column at last crossed the Manzanares and established positions in the yet-unfinished buildings of the University City on Madrid's north-west periphery. From the 17th to the 23rd, first the 6th Bandera, then the 4th, fought with the Red militia for possession of the seven floors of the Clinical Hospital, room by room and floor by floor, fighting with grenades and bayonets amid the stench of unburied corpses. By 23 November, when the hospital was finally secured, the 4th Bandera had suffered 250 casualties. That day Franco took the decision to halt the frontal attack on Madrid, which was costing too many lives, and instead instigated a plan of encirclement.

Expansion of the Legion

Between September 1936 and April 1938 12 new banderas were formed. The 7th and 8th (previously disbanded in 1932) were re-formed in September 1936. The 9th Bandera was formed in December 1936, the 10th in January 1937, the 11th and 12th in February 1937, the 13th in July 1937, the 14th and 15th in August 1937, the 16th in October 1937, the 17th in January 1938 and the 18th in April 1938.

Other Legion units were created during this period. Many Legion personnel were involved in the formation of the Nationalists' first Tank Company in October 1936, supplied with 15 Italian Fiat-Ansaldo L3/35 light tanks (3.2 tons—two 8 mm MGs). This company was expanded and became the Legion Tank Bandera by the beginning of 1937; initially it had two companies, each with 15 German Krupp Panzer IA tanks (5.4 tons—two 7.92 mm MGs), and was incorporated into the Nationalists' Tank Regiment No. 2 in November of that year.

Early in 1938 the Legion Light Tank Group was constituted, with headquarters at Dar Riffien, containing two banderas of three companies, each with 15 tanks. The 1st, 2nd, 4th and 5th Companies had Panzer IA and IB (6 tons, Maybach motor) tanks, and the 3rd and 6th Companies were supplied with captured Russian T-26Bs (9.2 tons—45 mm cannon and 7.62 mm MG). During the big tank battles of Alfambra, Aragón and Ebro the Group lost a total of 54 tanks and sustained numerous casualties. An Anti-Tank Company was formed in March 1937, as was a Flamethrower Company with two platoons of light flamethrowers and one of heavy, with nine teams in each platoon.

On 8 May 1937 the Tercio was, at last, officially denominated as the Legion, and the existing Legion groupings were now named 1st and 2nd Tercios. (Those banderas created during the war were not incorporated into either of the tercios.) In August 1937 a Depôt Bandera was established in Talavera to serve as a base for creating new banderas and to replace the severe losses of those in existence.

Portuguese volunteers, known as 'Viriatos', arrived in the Nationalist Zone in their hundreds early in the war and were mostly incorporated into banderas of the Legion, though never forming their own unit. The French, on the other hand, had their own 'Joan of Arc' Company which, in February 1938, constituted the 67th Company of the newly-raised 17th Bandera. For a brief six-month period there was an Irish Bandera—temporarily given the number 15—under the command of Gen. Eoin O'Duffy. The bandera had its own flag—an Irish wolfhound in saffron on a ground of emerald green—and the 600 personnel were permitted to wear Irish harp emblems on the lapels of their tunics. Though the Irish volunteers conducted themselves bravely during an advance under heavy

1: Corporal, 1921-27
2: Lieutenant, 1921-27
3: Legionary, 1921-25
4: Standard, 1st Bandera

A

1: Standard-bearer, 5 Oct. 1927
2: Legion national standard, 1927-31
3: Comandante, Oct. 1934

B

1: Col. Juan Yagüe, Sept. 1936
2: Lt. Col. Francisco Franco, May 1924
3: Brig. Gen. Millán Astray, 1937

1: Legionary, 1936
2: Captain, Tank Bandera, 1937
3: Sergeant, 1938

2

1

3

D

1: Colonel, 1945
2: Lieutenant-Colonel, 1945
3-6: Command flags, Tercios 1, 2, 3, 4

3

1

2

4

5

6

E

1: Legionary, 1957-58
2: Captain, 13th Independent Bandera, 1958
3: Legionary of a Saharan Tercio, 1966-70

1: Standard-bearer, 2nd Bdra., 1st Tercio, 1980
2: Lieutenant, 5th Bdra., 2nd Tercio, 1970
3: Pioneer corporal, 4th Bdra., 2nd Tercio, 1973

G

1: Legionary, 1975
2: Lieutenant, Special Ops., 1984
3: Corporal, Special Ops., 1984

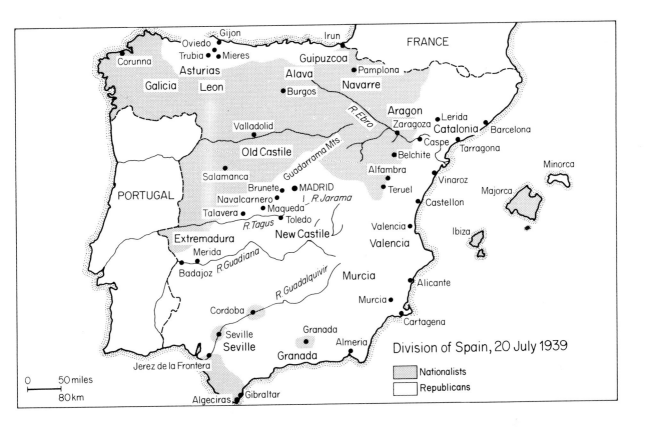

Map labels:

FRANCE

Corunna
Gijon
Oviedo
Trubia · · Mieres
Irun
Guipuzcoa
Pamplona
Asturias
Alava
Galicia
Leon
Navarre
Burgos
Aragon
Zaragoza
Lerida
Catalonia
Barcelona
Valladolid
Caspe
Tarragona
Old Castile
Guadarrama Mts.
Belchite
R. Ebro
Alfambra
Minorca
Salamanca
Teruel
Vinaroz
PORTUGAL
Brunete · MADRID
Majorca
Navalcarnero
R. Jarama
Castellon
Talavera · Maqueda
R. Tagus Toledo
Ibiza
Extremadura
New Castile
Valencia
Merida
Valencia
R. Guadiana
Badajoz
Murcia
R. Guadalquivir
Alicante
Cordoba
Murcia
Granada
Cartagena
Seville
Almeria
Seville
Granada
Jerez de la Frontera
Algeciras · Gibraltar

0   50 miles
     80 km

Division of Spain, 20 July 1939

Nationalists
Republicans

shell-fire near Ciempozuelos on 13 March 1937, the bandera was never effectively employed at the front, and returned to Ireland in June, having lost 15 dead. There were also small numbers of White Russians and Germans distributed amongst the Legion's predominantly Spanish ranks, and just a few British early in the war.

Nearly all of the Legion's officers during the war were Spanish. Four notable exceptions were British-Irish: Lieutenants Noel Fitzpatrick and William Nangle, both former British army officers, who served with the 5th Bandera; Alférez (Ensign) Peter Kemp, fresh from Cambridge University, who fought in the 14th Bandera and was wounded four times; and Cecil Owen (half-Spanish) who was killed at the battle of the Ebro in August 1938 while serving with the 16th Bandera.

Between January 1937 and April 1939 the Legion's banderas were active on nearly all of the principal battle fronts as follows (not always for total period):

1937

January–December. Defending the Madrid-Toledo front. Banderas 1, 4, 5, 6, 7, 8, 9, 10, 12 and 14.

3 January: Four Nationalist columns attacked north-west of Madrid to cut the Corunna road. Las Rozas occupied on 4th, Pozuelo de Alarcón on 7th and Aravaca on 8th. Banderas 5, 6, 7, 8 and 9.
6 February: Five reinforced Nationalist brigades attacked south of Madrid towards the Valencia road, capturing Marañosa and Ciempozuelos on 6th. Three columns crossed the Jarama river on 11th, opposed by four Republican divisions. Heaviest fighting was on a hill complex called the Pingarrón. Banderas 1, 4, 5, 6, 7, 8, 10, 11 and 12.
April–December: Operations in Andalusia. Bandera 11.
13 April: Republican attack on Corunna road, north-west of Madrid. Bandera 4.
July: Operations on Aragón front. Banderas 1, 2, 4 and 13.
5 July: Three Republican corps attacked Brunete, west of Madrid, aimed at Navalcarnero and the Extremadura road. Troops endured intense heat and thirst. Four Nationalist divisions recaptured Brunete on 26th. Estimated total casualties: Nationalists 14,000–15,000; Republicans 24,000–25,000. Banderas 1, 8 and 13.
24 August: Republican offensive in Aragón. Belchite

A rifle squad of the 4th Bandera occupies a communication trench near Navalcarnero on 21 October 1936. Note cylindrical German-type gas-mask container and Model 1913 Simson bayonets. (Keystone Press)

occupied on *6 September*. Banderas 1, 2, 4, 13 and 15.

9 September: Nationalist breakthrough in central sector in Asturias, over rugged mountain terrain. Cavadonga captured on *1 October*, Gijón occupied on 21st. Bandera 3.

15 December: 100,000 Republican troops assembled in Aragón. Three corps—40,000 men—launched attack and surrounded Teruel, defended by 10,000 Nationalists, by 22nd. Eight Nationalist divisions counter-attacked on 24th. Offensive was halted on 31st due to worst weather conditions for 20 years; thousands of men on both sides were victims of frostbite; many froze to death. Banderas 3, 13 and 15.

1938

January–December: Defending the Madrid–Toledo front. Banderas 5, 8, 9, 10, 12 and 16.

January–June: Operations in Andalusia. Bandera 11.

8 January: Republicans captured Teruel. Nationalist counter-offensive against Teruel was resumed on 10th. Battle of Alfambra commenced on 5

February and Nationalists crossed the Alfambra river on 17th. Teruel recaptured by Nationalists on 22nd. Banderas 1, 3, 4, 5, 6, 7, 13, 14 and 16.

9 March: Nationalist offensive in Aragón. Six corps advanced rapidly, occupying Belchite on 10th, Caspe on 17th, Lérida on *3 April* and reaching Vinaroz, on the Mediterranean coast, on 15th, cutting Republican territory in two. Nearly 200,000 Republican troops were cut off in Catalonia. Banderas 2, 3, 4, 5, 6, 7, 13, 14, 15, 16 and 17.

22 May: Nationalist operations in the Levante to follow up the above success, aimed at Valencia. Castellón occupied on *14 June*. Banderas 1, 2, 3, 4, 5, 6, 7, 13, 14, 15, 16 and 17.

25 July: Republican offensive across the River Ebro halted the Nationalist drive towards Valencia. 100,000 Republican troops were in the field. Two corps initially crossed to the right bank and captured 270 miles of territory from three Nationalist divisions in six days. Troops suffered effects of heat and thirst in very arid terrain. Nationalist counter-attacks ruptured the Republican front on *3 September* and finally captured heavily defended positions on high ridges called the Pandols and the Caballs between *30 October–2 November*. Republicans were driven back to the left bank by 16th. Total casualties: Nationalists 40,000; Republicans 70,000. Banderas 1, 2, 3, 4, 5, 6, 7, 11, 14, 16, 17 and 18.

23 December: 300,000 men, in seven Nationalist corps, advanced into Catalonia. Opposed by 140,000 Republicans.

1939

Nationalists captured Tarragona on *15 January* and Barcelona on 26th. The whole of Catalonia was occupied by *10 February*. 70,000 Republican troops were taken prisoner. Banderas 2, 3, 4, 5, 6, 7, 13, 14, 15, 16, 17 and 18.

March: 400,000 Republicans were still under arms in central Spain and the Levante. Nationalists marched into Madrid unopposed on 28th. On 30th they advanced without resistance to Alicante and Valencia. Almería, Murcia and Cartagena were occupied on 31st. Nationalists had reached their final objectives. Sector between Somosierra and the Levante—Banderas 1, 13, 14, 15, 16, 17 and 18. Madrid–Toledo front—Banderas 3, 5, 7, 8 and 12. Córdoba front—Banderas 4, 6, 10 and 11. In reserve—Banderas 2 and 9.

These brief facts and figures encompass many desperate combats, of which there is space here to mention only a handful:

12 February 1937: Legionaries of the 1st Bandera on the Jarama front, embattled against 19 Russian tanks, finally destroyed five with grenades, bottles of petrol and dynamite.

17 February 1937: The 8th Bandera resisted the attack of two International Brigades upon Pingarrón hill (Jarama). The 29th Company fought to the last cartridge and the last grenade before falling back. With the arrival of the 30th Company the savage encounter was renewed, with the wounded firing from behind the bodies of the dead, until the Internationalists retreated under crossfire.

10–11 May 1937: The 6th Bandera withstood assault after assault by tanks and infantry upon its positions at the Toledo bridgehead, sustaining 475 casualties (more than two-thirds) in two days.

11 July 1937: In attack and counter-attack at Villafranca, during the Brunete offensive, the 13th Bandera was decimated to the extent that the senior surviving rank in the entire bandera was a 'brigada' (sergeant-major).

21 February 1938: Attacked by numerous tanks and three battalions of carabineers during the battle of Alfambra, the 6th Bandera, firing their machine guns from well-entrenched positions, routed the enemy, who left nearly 200 dead and wounded strewn before the wire, while the bandera sustained only three casualties.

11 March 1938: On the Aragón front, Cpl. Renato Zanardo of the Light Tank Group, after losing his hand in an explosion, directed his tank to the aid of another which had broken down and was surrounded by the enemy. He then drove $3\frac{1}{2}$ miles to reach his own lines.

22 September 1938: During the Ebro offensive, Lt. Borghesse de Borbón led the 11th Company, 4th Bandera, in an attack upon enemy trenches. Wounded in the leg, the lieutenant nonetheless leapt into a machine gun post and killed the gunner and two servers single-handed. He then used their machine gun to give covering fire for his advancing platoons. The Republicans, strongly reinforced, now fiercely counter-attacked. Lt. Borghesse de Borbón threw grenade after grenade at the oncoming waves of enemy, and despatched

attackers who got too close with his pistol. Then a grenade exploded at his feet, wounding him in the chest; but he continued to fight on, rousing his men with cries of '*Viva España! Viva la Legión!*' until he finally died.

Employed as shock troops in nearly every Nationalist offensive, the Legion's casualties were always high, but so was its morale. Gen. de Bda. Morala Casaña, a Civil War veteran of the Legion, described to the author how in the Tremp sector of the Catalonia front, on the night of 24 December 1938, the 13th Bandera was defending a house between the River Segre and the Urgel canal, with covering fire from the 9th Tabor of Melilla, positioned on the other bank of the river:

'During the night the Reds launched continuous attacks. It was very impressive to hear in the noise of the battle the hymns of the Legion sung by the heroic defenders, who were supported all the while by the fire of the 9th Tabor's machine guns.'

On 1 April 1939 Generalísimo Franco signed a communiqué declaring the war to be finally over. During two years and nine months the Legion had suffered 37,393 total casualties—7,645 dead, 28,972 wounded and 776 missing in a total of 3,042 actions. The 1st, 4th, 11th and 15th Banderas were each awarded a Collective Laureate Cross of St Ferdinand, and the 6th Bandera two such awards. Collective Military Medals were awarded to the 1st Bandera (two), 2nd (one), 3rd (two), 4th (two), 5th (three), 6th (two), 7th (two), 16th (one), 17th (one) and Flamethrower Company (one). Seven Individual Laureate Crosses and 155 Individual Military Medals were also awarded.

Ifni-Sahara: 1957-58

With the conclusion of the Civil War, Banderas 12 to 18 were disbanded and the Legion returned to its original habitat in the Moroccan Protectorate. A re-organisation of 21 December 1939 created an Inspection (administrative headquarters) and Depôt Company in Ceuta, a Central Recruiting Office in Madrid, and three tercios: *1st Tercio*—1st, 2nd, 3rd, 10th and 11th Banderas—HQ Tauima; *2nd Tercio*—4th, 5th and 6th Banderas—HQ Dar

Riffien; *3rd Tercio*—7th, 8th and 9th Banderas—HQ Larache. Each tercio also contained a heavy weapons Mixed Group of four companies: command HQ, infantry cannons (four guns of 65/16 mm calibre), anti-tank guns (12 guns of 45 mm calibre), and anti-aircraft machine guns (12 MGs of 20 mm calibre).

From 21 December 1943 the tercios were given the titles of heroes who had commanded the famous Spanish armies of the 16th and 17th centuries: the 1st Tercio was named 'Gran Capitán', the 2nd 'Duque de Alba' and the 3rd 'Don Juan de Austria'. On 1 July 1947 the disbandment of the 10th and 11th Banderas began. A Sub-Inspection was created on 12 August 1950 to generally supervise organisation; and, in October of that year a 4th Tercio was formed—titled 'Alejandro Farnesio'—which was eventually composed of reconstituted 10th, 11th and 12th Banderas and a Mixed Group, with HQ in Villa Sanjurjo.

Gen. Millán Astray died in Madrid, aged 74, on 1 January 1954. At his own request, his Legion cap and a single white glove were placed upon his coffin, and on his granite headstone was inscribed: 'Charity and pardon—Millán Astray—Legionary'.

The last campaign

The independence of Morocco was formally recognised by France on 2 March 1956 and by Spain on 7 April. Spain, however, retained the northern coastal enclaves of Ceuta and Melilla and the southern region of Ifni on the west coast. It was in the vast Saharan territory to the south of Ifni that a new 13th Independent Bandera of the Legion established its headquarters at El Aaiún in July 1956. Fully organised by December, this bandera had a command headquarters, three rifle companies, and a company of machine guns, mortars and infantry cannons. It was linked initially to the 2nd Tercio, and later to the 3rd, for administrative purposes only.

Activists of the Moroccan extremist Istiqlal party had for some time been fomenting unrest and carrying out terrorist acts, both in Ifni and in the Saharan territory. The 13th Bandera was consequently deployed to desert posts in the interior, as was the 4th Bandera when it arrived in June 1957.

Legionaries of the 2nd Bandera quench their thirst in a pool after marching for 72 hours across the Saguia desert in the Spanish Sahara between 13 and 15 February 1958. (Agencia Efe)

The 2nd and 6th Banderas made a timely arrival in November.

During the night of 22/23 November 1957 some 2,500 Moroccan irregulars of the 'Sahara Liberation Army' (few of them actually natives of Ifni-Sahara), well-armed with automatic weapons and mortars, launched attacks from the Agadir region which encircled and isolated the Spanish frontier posts and practically surrounded the capital, Sidi-Ifni. On 4 December the 6th Bandera marched to the relief of the besieged fort of Tiliuin and, the following day, while under fire, evacuated all military and civil personnel to Sidi-Ifni, which they reached on the 6th. By the beginning of December 8,000 Spanish troops concentrated in Sidi-Ifni had staved off the threat to the capital, and the interior garrisons had been evacuated to their coastal bases. The units of the Legion—reinforced in February 1958 by the 9th Bandera—now undertook counter-insurgency operations in which they marched across miles of burning desert, often with no sign of an enemy. When finally encountered, the rebels would fight for a few hours and then disappear into the vast wilderness. In most of the actions fought the Legion's casualties were light, but there was one engagement with more serious results.

At 7 am on 13 January 1958 the 13th Bandera set out from El Aaiún to carry out a reconnaissance in the Edchera zone. The 2nd Company, in vanguard, was suddenly confronted at about 10.15 am by a well-positioned rebel force, about 500 strong, on the eastern margin of the dry bed of the wide Saguia el Hamra watercourse. In a manoeuvre to cover the left flank of the 2nd Company, the 1st Company advanced to the edge of the Saguia. The company commander, Capt. Jaúregui, now moved forward in his command car with his HQ personnel, and was killed when surprised by enemy fire.

Advancing into the dunes of the Saguia, the 3rd Platoon was ambushed by a rebel band. Attacked from the front and flank by an enemy at least three times their number, the 31 legionaries of the 3rd Platoon took up defensive positions. The platoon commander, Brigada (Sgt. Maj.) Fadrique, was wounded in the shoulder and in the left ear as he directed his men in constant close-quarter and hand-to-hand fighting which drove back numerous rebel attacks. After sustaining more than 50 per cent casualties, Brigada Fadrique ordered the survivors

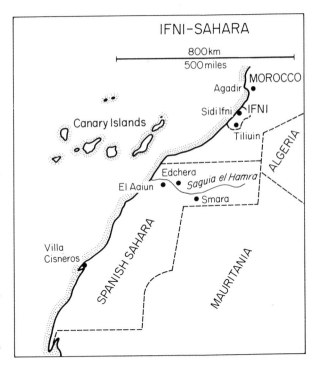

IFNI-SAHARA

to withdraw, carrying their wounded.

Remaining behind with only two corporals and a light machinegunner to cover the retreat, the brigada finally ordered the two corporals also to retire. Wounded once more in the leg, Brigada Fadrique, armed with a sub-machine gun, and Legionary Maderal, clutching his light machine gun, faced a final rush of Moroccan rebels, firing to the last and yelling 'Viva la Legión!' Struck by bullets in the stomach and head, Brigada Fadrique fell dead, as did Legionary Maderal at his side. For their valour both would be posthumously awarded the Laureate Cross of St Ferdinand. More than 30 rebel bodies were later found strewn around their position.

Under continuous bombardment from the deployed bandera's mortars and small arms, the enemy force broke contact during the night. In a reconnaissance at dawn the legionaries were able to recover their dead. The bandera had sustained 37 dead and 50 wounded in this action, and had killed 241 rebels.

Also threatened in its neighbouring Saharan territories of Mauritania and Algeria, the French government had now decided to co-operate with the Spanish in joint operations to defeat the 'Sahara Liberation Army'. During February 1958 French and Spanish aircraft launched bombing and rocket attacks upon enemy supply centres and caravans, while 9,000 Spanish and 5,000 French troops flushed out the rebels on the ground.

Commencing on 10 February, 'Motorised Group A'—composed of the 4th, 9th and 13th Banderas, the Santiago Cavalry Regiment and an infantry battalion, plus artillery, mortars, and other supporting elements—occupied the Edchera Pass on the Saguia el Hamra, drove on to Tafurdat and finally, on the 20th, captured the rebel stronghold at Smara in conjunction with French forces from Fort Trinquet. By early March the combined offensive of Spanish Motorised Groups and French columns had effectively defeated the 'Sahara Liberation Army'. The region was now considered

pacified. Legion casualties in this campaign were 55 dead, 74 wounded and one missing.

In August 1958 Tercios 3 and 4 were moved to the Spanish Sahara, with headquarters in El Aaiún and Villa Cisneros respectively, and were consequently to be known as Saharan Tercios. By October the two tercios were constituted as follows: *Saharan Tercio 'Don Juan de Austria', 3rd of the Legion*—7th and 8th Banderas, 1st Light Armoured Group and a Motorised Battery. *Saharan Tercio 'Alejandro Farnesio', 4th of the Legion*—9th and 10th Banderas, 2nd Light Armoured Group and a Motorised Battery.

The two light armoured groups (from 1 January 1966 retitled 1st and 2nd Light Saharan Groups) were each composed of a Headquarters Squadron and 1st and 2nd Light Squadrons. Each group was originally equipped with five American M24 Chaffee light tanks (20.3 tons—75 mm cannon, two

Standard-bearers of the Legion attend the inauguration of a monument to Gen. Millán Astray in his birthplace, Corunna, on 20 September 1970, as part of the celebrations to commemorate the 50th anniversary of the founding of the Legion. (Agencia Efe)

7.62 mm MGs and one 12.70 mm MG) and 12 M8 Greyhound armoured cars (37 mm cannon, one 7.62 mm MG and one 12.70 mm MG). In January 1966 these vehicles were replaced by French Panhard AML-245 armoured cars, each group receiving six AML-90s (90/33 mm cannon and one 7.62 mm MG) and 12 AML-60s (60 mm breach-loading mortar and two 7.62 mm MGs). In 1970 the 1st Light Saharan Group was equipped with 19 French AMX-30 medium tanks (36 tons—105/56 mm cannon, one 7.62 mm MG and one 12.7 mm MG) and, from 1974, French Panhard M3/VTT armoured transports (two 7.62 mm MGs) were supplied to both groups.

The Motorised Batteries each had four howitzers of 105/11 mm calibre mounted in Canadian GMC-15TA armoured transports. An army re-organisation at the beginning of 1964 disbanded these batteries.

The 1st Company, 4th Bandera marches past in Madrid in June 1973 during Franco's annual Victory Parade; as witnessed by the author, the Legion was warmly applauded by the large crowds lining the route. The company *banderín*—small flag—displays the red Burgundy cross on a yellow ground.

(Below)
A motorised detachment of the June 1973 parade. The officer standing in the vehicle at far right holds the standard of the 2nd Tercio, showing on its reverse side the Legion emblem on a black ground bordered with yellow. (Author's photo)

End of a Mission: 1961-76

With Moroccan independence, the Legion's mission in the Protectorate drew to a close. On 28 February 1961 the 4th Bandera handed over to the Royal Moroccan Army the beautiful quarters and gardens of the Legion's first depôt at Dar Riffien, founded by Franco and his 1st Bandera more than 40 years before. That same day the 3rd Bandera relinquished the equally lovely base at Tauima. The 1st and 2nd Tercios now moved to their new headquarters in the retained Spanish coastal enclaves of Melilla and Ceuta.

Both Morocco and Mauritania laid claim to the Spanish Sahara, but there were few internal disorders in the territory during the 1960s. The 13th Bandera was disbanded in June 1969, following the transfer of Ifni to Morocco. In the early 1970s there were sporadic disturbances in the Spanish Sahara, during which the Legion suffered only three casualties. An acute crisis arose in October 1975 when the Moroccan King Hassan II organised the 'Green March' of 250,000 unarmed people, who marched from Agadir with the expressed intention of peacefully occupying the Saharan territory. The 3rd Tercio, based at El Aaiún, and the 4th, at Edchera (HQ still at Villa Cisneros in the south), stood ready behind the border minefields. Fortunately, at the last moment, the marchers turned back; and on 11 November the Spanish government passed a law to decolonise their Saharan territory, to take effect from 28 February 1976.

At 5.25 am on 20 November 1975 Francisco Franco died. Three days later the co-founder of the Legion—and the absolute ruler who had transformed a backward, strife-torn and poverty-stricken land into a modern nation which, if politically stagnant, at least enjoyed real peace and prosperity—was laid to rest in the basilica of the Valley of the Fallen in the Guadarrama mountains. Many legionaries and ex-legionaries were among the hundreds of thousands who attended both the lying-in-state and funeral ceremonies.

Withdrawal from the Sahara in February 1976 ended the Legion's mission in Spanish Africa, and meant the disbandment of the 4th Tercio. Despite calls from some quarters for its total abolition, the Legion survived to celebrate its 60th anniversary in September 1980 and, at the time of writing, still exists. It is deployed as follows: *Tercio 'Gran Capitán', 1st of the Legion*—1st, 2nd and 3rd Banderas—HQ Melilla; *Tercio 'Duque de Alba', 2nd of the Legion*—4th, 5th and 6th Banderas—HQ Ceuta; *Tercio 'Don Juan de Austria', 3rd of the Legion*—7th and 8th Banderas and 1st Light Group—HQ Fuerteventura, Canary Islands.

During recent decades volunteers for the Legion have been largely young Spaniards who prefer a two-year enlistment in this élite corps to serving 18 months 'mili'-conscription. 'Foreign' elements—who must enlist for the normal three years—have been principally from the European continent and black Africa, with a very few Americans and British (who sometimes have been unable to accept the hard life, and have tried to desert). As stated in a Legion recruiting pamphlet—'Here there is only room for the valiant!'

The Saharan 4th Tercio 'Alejandro Farnesio', in camouflage-patterned uniforms, parades in honour of the Captain-General of the Canary Islands during his visit to Edchera, Spanish Sahara in 1975. (Agencia Efe)

The Plates

A1: Corporal, 1921–27

This is the Legion's first regulation campaign uniform of khaki-green 'guerrera' tunic, and 'granadero' breeches buttoning from knee to ankle. The sandals originally worn were soon discarded in favour of the white canvas ankle-boots (alpargatas) worn by the Moroccan Regulares. Three red chevrons of rank are displayed diagonally on the corporal's lower sleeves and vertically on the right side of his 'isabelino' forage cap—so named after the caps worn by the soldiers of Queen Isabel II. The cap is piped in red, with a red tassel on the forward peak. The Legion's emblem of pike, harquebus and cross-bow with a crown superimposed— representing the arms used by the Spanish tercios of the 16th and 17th centuries—is displayed on the shoulder-straps. Canvas Mills equipment, used in World War I, was purchased from the British in Gibraltar. His rifle is the 1913 version of the Spanish 7 mm Model 93 Mauser.

A2: Lieutenant, 1921–27

Wearing the same basic uniform, and with an officer's set of Mills equipment, this lieutenant has officer's red and gold piping and tassel on his 'isabelino' cap. His exact rank—teniente—is shown by the two six-pointed gold stars beneath a crown on the front of the cap and on each of his cuffs. He has gold piping on his shoulder-straps; the collar of the grey-green shirt is worn outside the tunic. His holstered pistol would be a Spanish 9 mm Astra Model 400 automatic, with an eight-round magazine.

A3: Legionary, 1921–25

Summer campaign uniform consisted of the grey-green shirt with rolled sleeves; khaki-green breeches, worn by this legionary with puttees wound around the lower legs; and white canvas boots. Note that the original Legion shirt had neither pockets nor shoulder-straps, both of which were added in 1926. The green drill slouch hat, with the Legion emblem embroidered on the front, gave good protection from the sun. In his ammunition pouches the legionary would have 210 cartridges (as opposed to the normal infantry supply of 150) for

Command bugler of the Saharan 3rd Tercio 'Don Juan de Austria' sounds a call on the 'cornetín' (small bugle) at El Aaiún, Spanish Sahara in 1975. Behind the three red corporal's tapes above his pocket is a patch with a Burgundy cross in white and black, indicating that his unit is Headquarters, 3rd Tercio. (Agencia Efe)

his five-shot M93 rifle, complete with Model 1913 Simson bayonet. Cold rations were carried in a side-pack, and on longer operations he would carry a rolled blanket and individual tent slung, bandolier-fashion, from right shoulder to left side.

A4: Standard of the 1st Bandera

On a black ground is the coat-of-arms of the House of Burgundy—two wild boars biting an oak bough. Battle honours are recorded on ribbons suspended from the spearhead.

B1: Standard-bearer, 5 October 1927

This lieutenant is depicted at the ceremony at Dar Riffien when Queen Victoria Eugenia presented the Legion with its first national standard. He wears khaki-green parade uniform, with three gold wound chevrons displayed on his left upper sleeve. From left shoulder to right side is slung a red and

Field Mass in the barracks of the 3rd Tercio in Fuerteventura, Canary Islands during a visit by President Suarez in 1978. Note the ram mascot near the far left. (Agencia Efe)

gold bandolier and 'bucket' to support the standard. The bandolier covers the decorations on his chest, but identifiable is the Cross of Maria Cristina on his left pocket. Note the large spur-leathers of antique design, recalling the fashion of the 17th century.

B2: The Legion's first national standard, 1927–31

The Queen of Spain and her ladies-in-waiting embroidered this red and gold national standard. In the two top corners are shown the royal ciphers of King Alfonso XIII and Queen Victoria Eugenia, and in the bottom corners the two Collective Military Medals awarded to the entire Legion for distinguished actions in the Melilla region in July 1921 and from 28 May to 5 June 1923. Surrounding the royal coat-of-arms is embroidered the Legion's rallying-cry 'Legionaries to fight—legionaries to die'.

B3: Comandante, October 1934

The rank of *comandante* (major) is shown by the eight-pointed gold star on the front of the red-and-gold-piped '*isabelino*', which has a gold tassel. Since the advent of the Republic in 1931 the royal crown was removed from officers' caps and from the Legion's emblem, which is shown here on a diamond-shaped patch on the *comandante*'s chest

and also on the metal buckle plate of his brown leather belt. The left upper sleeve of his grey jersey—a very suitable piece of field uniform in the cold climate of Asturias during the October revolution—displays two gold wound chevrons, while the lower sleeve bears the badge of the Collective Military Medal.

C1: Colonel Juan Yagüe, September 1936

Depicted at the time of his appointment as Colonel Inspector of the Legion, he is clad in grey-green Legion shirt—now with pleated pockets and shoulder straps—light khaki breeches and black boots. Yagüe displays the Legion emblem on the buckle-plate of his belt; and the three eight-pointed gold stars of a *coronel*, both on his red-and-gold-piped, gold-tasselled cap and on the black patch—'galleta'—above his left pocket.

C2: Lieutenant-Colonel Francisco Franco, May 1924

Portrayed here as commanding officer of the Legion, mounted on his white horse *en route* to relieve the encircled outpost of Tizzi Asa, Franco wears the two eight-pointed gold stars of *teniente coronel* both on his cap and on his cuff beneath the badge of the Collective Military Medal. A Moorish turban is worn as a desert scarf.

C3: Brigadier-General José Millán Astray, 1937

Retaining the title of Honorary Colonel of the Legion, Millán Astray wears an '*isabelino*' with the gold piping, tassel and embroidery of his general's rank, and has the Legion emblem on the shoulder straps of his shirt. On his chest, from left to right, are pinned the Individual Military Medal; the Medal of Suffering for the Country, for those wounded by enemy fire (of which he had a special award bordered in diamonds) with four clasps; and the Mutilated by War for the Country award—only three of the many decorations to which he was entitled. Around his waist is his general's red sash with gold tassels.

D1: Legionary, 1936

With the outbreak of the Civil War the Legion emblem began to appear on the front of the forage cap. Otherwise summer campaign uniform remained the same as had been worn in Morocco. The Spanish Model 93 Mauser rifle was still the usual weapon, largely replaced later in the war by Czech 7.92 mm Mauser carbines taken from the enemy. Brown leather ammunition pouches and belts had begun to replace the canvas Mills equipment during the Alhucemas operations of 1925. An aluminium water-bottle in a green cloth cover is worn at the right hip. The leather strap adorned with bullets, worn around the legionary's left wrist, was a popular and purely ornamental affectation.

D2: Captain, Tank Bandera, 1937

In summer 'walking out' uniform, this officer wears the black beret with silver metal skull-and-crossbones badge of all Nationalist armoured units, and above his right breast pocket is the silver metal badge of tank personnel. The three six-pointed gold stars of a *capitán* are displayed on the black patch above his left pocket. Otherwise he wears the grey-green shirt, green breeches, black leather boots and white gloves of Legion officers in the infantry banderas.

D3: Sergeant, 1938

In February 1938 a new winter campaign uniform was issued, consisting of a short 'cazadora' blouse, which buttoned to the neck and at the wrists, and 'bombacho' trousers, which fastened above the ankles, both of green serge. The *sargento* depicted also wears the normal forage cap. The leather equipment is now black, as are the new calf-length leather boots,

Lt.Gen. Merry Gordon inspects the 2nd Tercio in Ceuta on 20 September 1980, during a ceremony to celebrate the 60th anniversary of the founding of the Legion. (Agencia Efe)

with two-strap upper flaps buckling outside the ankle. His sergeant's insignia of three gold tapes is shown above his left breast pocket and also on the right side of his forage cap, while on his left upper sleeve is the shield of the 150th Moroccan Division. The sub-machine gun is a Spanish copy of the German 9 mm MP 28 II (rate of fire 600 rounds per minute).

E1: Colonel, 1945

A leather chin-strap was added to the forage cap soon after the Civil War, first by the motorised units, then by the entire Legion. This colonel is dressed in green service uniform, with his three eight-pointed gold rank stars shown on the gold-piped cuffs of his tunic, which also bears the Legion emblem on the gold-edged shoulder-straps. On the right breast pocket can be seen the metal and enamel emblem of the *Regulares*, in which corps the colonel has previously served for 14 years, as shown by the 'permanency bars' beneath the emblem—two gold (five years each) and four red (one year each). Permanency bars—similarly added to the Legion emblem—were worn only by personnel who had seen action with the unit concerned.

The 2nd Tercio marches past Lt.Gen. Merry Gordon (taking the salute) in Ceuta. Note Z-70B sub-machine guns slung diagonally across the men's backs. (Agencia Efe)

E2: Lieutenant-Colonel, 1945

Full dress uniforms for officers and warrant officers were coloured khaki from 1943. This senior officer wears the 'teresiana' cap—originally that of the light infantry battalions, but adopted by the Legion during its formative period for 'walking out' and parades—which has piping, a strap and a button at the front above crossed rifles with an eight-pointed rank star on each side, all in gold. On his left upper sleeve is a gold wound chevron, and on the forearm the badge of the Collective Military Medal. The Legion emblem is shown on the red diamond-shaped metal badges on his collar points. On his right upper sleeve is the red and gold shield worn by veterans of the Spanish 'Blue Division' which fought in Russia from 1941–43[1]. This also explains the Iron Cross 1st Class on his right breast pocket. Decorations on his left breast are (left to right) the Individual Military Medal; the Medal of Suffering

[1]See MAA 103, *Germany's Spanish Volunteers 1941–45*

for the Country (wounded by enemy fire) with one clasp; the Campaign Medal 1936–39; and the Blue Division Campaign Medal. Below is the War Cross 1936–39. The gold waist belt, authorised in 1943, displays the emblem of the Spanish Ground Forces on the buckle plate and supports his sword, while from right shoulder to left side is slung the red Sash of Victory, authorised in 1940 to commemorate the 1936–39 'Crusade'. This uniform is worn with a white shirt and black tie.

E3, 4, 5 and 6 illustrate the command flags of Tercios 1, 2, 3 and 4 respectively.

F1: Legionary, 1957–58

Commencing operations in Ifni-Sahara in November 1957, legionaries wore the new green *tabardo* coat with gold buttons, first authorised in 1955, with grey-green trousers and white canvas boots. The Legion emblem is shown on the forage cap, on the red metal badges on the coat collar points, and on the gold buckle plate of the waist belt. The black leather belt across his chest supports a satchel slung on the back. He is armed with a Spanish 9 mm Star Model Z-45 sub-machine gun (rate of fire 400–500 rpm).

F2: Captain, 13th Independent Bandera, 1958
In grey-green shirt and breeches and black leather boots, this officer wears a green visored cap with a pale green 'siroquera' cloth, worn as protection against the fierce, hot, south-east wind called the 'sirocco', which fills the mouth, nose, ears and eyes with sand—hence also the goggles. The three six-pointed gold stars of captain's rank are worn above his left pocket on a green patch with a red diagonal Burgundy cross, indicating that his unit is the 13th Independent Bandera. His pistol is the Spanish 9 mm Super Star which has a nine-round magazine.

F3: Legionary, Saharan Tercio, 1966–70
This legionary of the 3rd or 4th Tercio wears a green visored cap and 'siroquera', with goggles fastened around the crown; a grey-green shirt, green shorts and stockings, light brown open-toed sandals, and black leather equipment with a gold buckle plate bearing the Legion's emblem. The small leather 'lengüeta' ('tongue') suspended from the button of the right pocket displays a legionary's head and Legion emblem. These adornments became popular in the Saharan Tercios around 1966, and there were soon many unit varieties. His

rifle is the Spanish CETME Model 58, with a 20-round detachable box magazine (rate of fire: single shots 40 rpm; up to 650 rpm on fully automatic).

G1: Standard-bearer, 2nd Bandera, 1st Tercio 'Gran Capitán', 1980
Summer parade uniform for this sergeant consists of normal Legion forage cap and shirt, Model 1973 trousers with two flapped side pockets on each leg, canvas belts, white gloves, and black leather calf-length boots now with three buckled straps at the side. His three gold tapes of rank are displayed on a red (colour of the 2nd Bandera) patch above his left breast pocket, and on the right side of his cap. The Legion emblem (with a crown once more, since the coronation of King Juan Carlos in November 1975) is shown on his cap and shoulder straps. On his right upper sleeve is the shield of the 1st Tercio. His red and gold bandolier, with 'bucket', is slung from his left shoulder to his right side. The flag of the 2nd Bandera comprises the coat-of-arms of the House of Habsburg—a black double-headed eagle on a red ground. This emblem is also displayed on his leather 'lengüeta'.

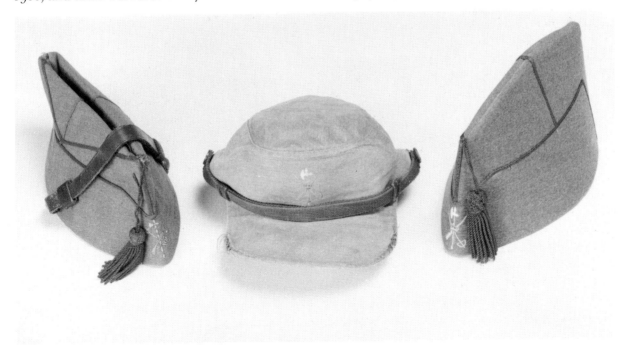

(Left) 'Isabelino' forage cap from the period following the Civil War. (Centre) Visored cap, post-1975, of type first introduced during the campaign of Ifni-Sahara. (Right) Recent example of forage cap. All three display the Legion emblem with (centre and right) a royal crown. (Author's collection)

Collectors of militaria should note that the shield on the right sleeve, and the rank patch above the left pocket identify this shirt to a lieutenant of the Legion's Special Operations Unit (see Plate H2). The metal Special Operations course badge pinned on the left pocket is normally worn above the right pocket. Displayed there instead is a parachutist's brevet, showing that the lieutenant is a former paratrooper. However, the wearing of the Parachute Brigade emblem on the left sleeve is anomalous, and the metal badge for 25 parachute jumps, above the rank patch, should in fact be worn on the left upper sleeve. The '*lengüeta*' on the right pocket correctly displays the emblem of the Sub-Inspection of the Legion. (Author's collection)

G2: Lieutenant, 5th Bandera, 2nd Tercio 'Duque de Alba', 1970

Note two six-pointed gold rank stars on the front of his '*isabelino*', which also displays the company-grade officer's red and gold piping and tassel; and on the yellow (colour of the 5th Bandera) patch above his left breast pocket. This lieutenant wears a light grey-green summer 'campaign and manoeuvres' uniform and black leather belts, holster and buckled boots. Note that, even on manoeuvres, a Legion officer wears white gloves. Slung on his back, over his pack, is a rolled canvas campaign tent.

G3: Pioneer Corporal, 4th Bandera, 2nd Tercio 'Duque de Alba', June 1973

Each bandera has a pioneer squad consisting of a corporal and six legionaries (1st class). Marching in the annual Civil War victory parade in Madrid, this pioneer corporal of the 4th Bandera wears summer parade uniform, a black leather belt with gold Legion emblem on the buckle plate, and a black leather bandolier to support the hand-saw slung behind his right shoulder. (Pioneer legionaries carry picks or shovels.) The three red tapes of his rank are worn on the right side of his cap and on the red (colour of the 4th Bandera) patch above his left breast pocket. The ornamental shoulder-knots of red braided and tasselled cords pass from his left shoulder to his right. The oval metal plate on the bandolier shows the emblem of the 4th Bandera—the gold crucified Christ of Don Juan de Austria at the battle of Lepanto, on a red ground. This emblem appears again, with a gold Legion device, on a red background in a gold rim, on his left upper sleeve. On his right sleeve is the shield of the 2nd

Tercio. At this time (1973) the gauntlets of 4th Bandera pioneers were white, though they changed to red shortly after. His right shoulder supports a Spanish CETME Model 68 rifle, modified to take the NATO 7.62 mm round in place of the lighter round of the Model 58.

On parade the pioneers are accompanied by a ram mascot adorned with an embroidered blanket in the colour of the bandera, and with its horns and hooves gilded. The ram is not led, but walks free—in perfect step with the soldiers!

H1: Legionary, Saharan Tercio 1975
Camouflage-patterned uniforms were first worn by the Saharan Tercios at the beginning of 1975. Note that the visored cap is still green (as also was the 'siroquera', when worn, until late in that year). He wears black leather buckled boots, and webbing belts and ammunition pouches for his CETME Model 68 rifle. The only insignia worn is the Legion emblem on his cap.

H2: Lieutenant, Special Operations Unit, 1948
The Special Operations Unit, based in Ronda (Province of Málaga), has officially replaced the unofficial Special Operations Platoons (see H3). In summer 'formations and guards' uniform, this lieutenant is clad in forage cap, short-sleeved shirt and Model 1973 trousers, webbing belt and holster, black leather buckled boots and white gloves. On his right sleeve is the Legion Special Operations Unit shield and on his left the metal badge for 25 parachute jumps which, with his parachutist's brevet worn above the right pocket, shows the lieutenant to be an ex-paratrooper. Above the left pocket is a green patch bearing the Legion emblem and two gold rank stars. Pinned on his left pocket is the metal Special Operations course badge (officer's), while suspended from the button of the right pocket is a 'lengüeta' with the emblem of the Sub-Inspection (organisational HQ) of the Legion.

H3: Corporal, Special Operations Platoon, 1976

In about 1970, Special Operations Platoons were formed in the banderas on an unofficial basis, to train in guerrilla and counter-guerrilla warfare. This corporal displays the short 'camisola' blouse (worn by paratroops since 1955, and adopted by the Legion in their own green shade in 1967), and Model 1973 trousers. The Legion emblem is displayed on his visored cap and shoulder straps and on the green patch above his left breast pocket, which also bears the three red tapes of rank and his name. Being a former paratrooper entitles him to wear his parachutist's brevet above the right pocket. His webbing belt supports ammunition pouches for his Spanish 9 mm Star Z-70B sub-machine gun (rate of fire 550 rpm).

Notes sur les planches en couleur

A1 Premier modèle de l'uniforme de campagne. Notez l'insigne de la Légion sur les pattes d'épaule; insignes de rang sur l'avant-bras et le côté du calot et matériel de ceinturon et cartouchière en toile britannique de l'époque 1914–18. **A2** La lisière; le gland du calot permettent de reconnaître un officier; le rang exact est montré par les étoiles d'or du calot et des manchettes. **A3** Uniforme de campagne d'été, avec manches de chemise roulées et chapeau rabattu brodé de l'insigne de la Légion. **A4** Armoiries, Maison de Bourgogne.

B1 Uniforme de parade vert kaki, porté pour la cérémonie durant laquelle la Reine présenta le premier étendard de la Légion. Chevrons de blessé or sur la manche gauche. **B2** Etendard présenté durant cette cérémonie, avec les chiffres royaux d'Alfonse XIII et de Victoria Eugénie; médailles militaires collectives obtenues par la Légion au Maroc et devise de ralliement 'les légionnaires doivent se battre—les légionnaires doivent mourir'. **B3** Le rang est montré par l'étoile à huit branches du calot et le gland doré. Deux chevrons de blessé et la médaille militaire collective sont portés sur la manche du tricot gris, vêtement utile des campagnes d'hiver.

C1 Présenté au moment de sa nomination comme colonel-inspecteur de la Légion; l'écharpe kaki clair ne font pas partie de la tenue réglementaire de la Légion. **C2** Uniforme de campagne habituel, avec étoiles de rang sur le calot et les manchettes et un turban musulman porté comme écharpe de désert. **C3** Uniforme de Colonel Honoraire de la Légion; décorations de calot d'officier général, insigne de la Légion sur les pattes d'épaule, écharpe d'officier général et trois des médailles auxquelles il avait droit.

D1 L'insigne de la Légion est maintenant porté à l'avant du calot. L'équipement personnel en cuir remplace le type en toile de sangle à partir de 1925. L'uniforme est par ailleurs tel qu'il était durant la guerre du *Rif*. **D2** Uniforme 'de sortie' d'été, avec le béret, l'insigne de béret et l'insigne de poitrine des unités de choc ajoutés à l'uniforme de l'officier d'infanterie. **D3** Le nouvel uniforme de 1938: courte veste *cazadora* et pantalons larges et long *bombacho*, équipement en cuir noir et bottes à revers de cheville à boucle. Insigne de la 150e division marocaine sur la manche gauche.

E1 Jugulaire ajoutée au calot juste après la guerre civile. Cet officier, en uniforme de service ordinaire, porte sur le sein droit l'emblème des *Regulares*, avec des barrettes témoignant de 14 ans de service dans cette unité avant son transfert à la Légion. **E2** Tenue d'uniforme complète, avec képi *teresiana*, insignes de col de la légion et insignes de la manche droite des vétérans de la Division bleue de Russie, ce qui explique le mélange des décorations de la guerre civile espagnole et des décorations allemandes. **E3–6** Drapeaux des *Tercios* 1–4.

F1 Veste *tabardo* type 1933 avec insignes de la Légion sur le col. La courroie noire sur la poitrine soutient une besace sur le dos. L'arme est la mitraillette Star Z-45. **F2** 13e *Bandera* reconnue par les couleurs de l'écusson de poitrine qui porte les étoiles de rang. L'écharpe de tête de désert—'*siroquera*'—est portée sur le nouveau képi de campagne à visière. **F3** La 'languette' en cuir portée sur le sein droit, portant l'emblème de la Légion ou de l'unité, devint populaire à cette époque. L'arme est le fusil CETME M58.

G1 Uniforme de parade d'été, avec pantalons M1973 comportant des poches sur les jambes; les ornements de parade rouges permettent de reconnaître la 2e *Bandera*; insignes de manche de la 1ere *Tercio* et étendard de *Bandera*, avec armoiries de la Maison de Hapsbourg. **G2** Tenue des manœuvres d'été; notez l'écusson à fond jaune (5e *Bandera*) pour les étoiles de rang et les gants blancs portés même avec cet uniforme. **G3** Chaque *bandera* possède un escadron de pionniers de cérémonie consistant en un caporal—qui porte une scie—et six soldats portant des pioches et des pelles. Uniforme de parade d'été avec signes distinctifs des pionniers complexes, du rouge de cette *bandera*, et les insignes de manche du 2e *Tercio*.

H1 Les uniformes de camouflage firent leur apparition dans les *Tercios* du Sahara en 1975, portés avec le képi à visière vert notez les sangles en toile pour le fusil CETME M68. **H2** Tenue de service d'été. Sur la manche droite, l'insigne de peloton Opérations Spéciales de la Légion; sur le sein droit, 'ailes' de parachutiste, sur le sein gauche, écusson vert des unités d'Opérations Spéciales avec insigne de la Légion et étoiles de rang; au-dessous, insigne de qualification pour Opérations Spéciales. **H3** Blouse *camisola* portée dans le vert de la Légion depuis 1967; insigne de la Légion sur le képi à visière et pattes d'épaule; écusson de poitrine vert (Opérations Spéciales) portant le nom, les galons de rang et l'insigne de la Légion; insigne de parachutiste comme à H2. Notez la mitraillette Z-70B et les cartouchières pour celle-ci.

Farbtafeln

A1 Die erste offizielle Felduniform. Beachten Sie das Abzeichen der Legion auf den Schulterstreifen, die Ranginsignien auf dem Ärmel und auf der Feldmütze sowie die britische Gürtelpatronentasche aus Segeltuch aus den Jahren 1914–18. **A2** Rot-goldene Biesen und Quasten an der Feldmütze bezeichnen einen Offizier. Seinen genauen Rang erkennt man an den goldenen Sternen an der Feldmütze und an den Manschetten. **A3** Sommer-Feldzuguniform mit hochgekrempelten Hemdsärmeln und Hut mit aufgestecktem Legionsabzeichen. **A4** Wappen des Hauses Burgund.

B1 Khaki-grüne Paradeuniform, die Soldaten bei der Feier trugen, auf der die Königin die erste Nationalflagge der Legion überreichte. Am linken Ärmel goldene, gewundene Winkel. **B2** Die bei dieser Feier überreichte Flagge mit dem königlichen Monogramm von Alfonso XIII und Victoria Eugenia. Kollektiv-Militärmedaillen, die die Legion in Marokko errungen hat. Das Motto der Legion 'Legionäre, um zu kämpfen—Legionäre, um zu sterben'. **B3** Der achtzackige Stern auf der Feldmütze und die goldene Quaste zeigen den Rang an. Zwei gewundene Winkel und Kollektiv-Militärmedaille am Ärmel der grauen Jersey-Uniform, die für den Winter sehr praktisch war.

C1 Ein Soldat bei seiner Ernennung zum Oberstinspekteur der Legion. Die helle, khakifarbene Reithose gehört nicht zur regulären Legionsuniform. **C2** Die alte Feldzuguniform mit Rangsternen an Feldmütze und Manschetten und ein maurischer Turban, der als Wüstenschal dient. **C3** Die Uniform des Ehrenoberst der Legion: übliche Offiziersauszeichnungen an der Feldmütze, Legionsabzeichen an den Schulterstreifen, Offiziersschärpe und drei der vielen Medaillen, die er tragen durfte.

D1 Hier ist das Legionsabzeichen vorn auf der Feldmütze. Das persönliche Zubehör aus Leder ersetzte nach und nach das gewebte Material aus dem Jahre 1925. Sonst ist die Uniform dieselbe wie im *Rif*-Krieg. **D2** Sommer-Ausgeh-Uniform mit Béret, Kappenabzeichen und Brustabzeichen der Panzereinheit sowie Offiziersuniform der Infanterie. **D3** Die neue Uniform von 1938: kurze *Cazadora*-Jacke und lange, weite *Bombacho*-Hose, schwarze Lederausrüstung und Stiefel mit beschnallten Laschen. Insignien der 150. Marokkanischen Division am linken Ärmel.

E1 Kurz nach dem Bürgerkrieg eingeführte Feldmütze mit Kinnriemen. Dieser Offizier in normaler Uniform trägt das Emblem der *Regulares* rechts auf der Brust sowie Streifen, die 14 Jahre Dienstzeit bei dieser Einheit anzeigen, bevor er zur Legion kam. **E2** Volle Paradeuniform mit *Teresiana*-Mütze, Kragenabzeichen der Legion und Insignien der Veteranen der 'Blauen Division' in Russland am Ärmel, was die Mischung von deutschen und spanischen Bürgerkriegsauszeichnungen erklärt. **E3–6** Flaggen der 1.–4. *Tercios*.

F1 *Tabardo*-Jacke aus dem Jahre 1955, sowie Legionsabzeichen am Kragen. Der schwarze Riemen quer über der Brust hält eine Tasche auf dem Rücken. Die Waffe ist eine Star-Z45-Maschinenpistole. **F2** Die 13. *Bandera* erkennt man an den Farben des Brustabzeichens mit Rangsternen. Das Wüstenkopftuch '*Siroquera*' trugen Soldaten über der neuen Feldmütze mit Sichtschutz. **F3** Die lederne 'Zunge' auf der rechten Brust mit Emblem der Legion bzw. Einheit war zu diesem Zeitpunkt sehr beliebt. Die Waffe ist ein CETME-M58-Gewehr.

G1 Sommer-Paradeuniform mit M1973-Hose. Rote Paradeverzierung, typisch für die 2. *Bandera*. Ärmelinsignien der 1. *Tercio*, *Bandera*-Flagge sowie Wappen des Hauses Hapsburg. **G2** Sommer-Manöveruniform. Beachten Sie das gelbe Hintergrundabzeichen (5. *Bandera*) für Rangsterne sowie weisse Handschuhe. **G3** Jede *Bandera* hat eine zeremonielle Pionierschwadron, bestehend aus einem Obergefreiten, der die Säge trägt, sowie Soldaten mit Spitzhacke und Schaufel. Sommer-Paradeuniform mit Pioniersmerkmalen auf rotem Hintergrund dieser *Bandera* sowie Ärmelinsignien der 2. *Tercio*.

H1 Tarnuniform der *Tercios* 1975 in der Sahara mit grüner Feldmütze und Sichtschutz. Beachten Sie das gewebte Zubehor für das CETME-M68-Gewehr. **H2** Sommerdienstkleidung. Am rechten Ärmel Insignien des Zugs für Sonderaufgaben der Legion. Auf der Brust rechts 'Flügel' der Fallschirmjäger und links das Abzeichen der Einheit für Sonderaufgaben mit Legionsabzeichen und Rangsternen. Darunter Qualifikationsabzeichen für Sonderaufgaben. **H3** Grünes *Camisola*-Hemd, das die Legion seit 1967 trägt. Legionsabzeichen auf der Mütze mit Sichtschutz und auf den Schulterstreifen. Grünes Brustabzeichen (Sonderaufgaben) mit Name, Rangstreifen und Legionsabzeichen. Insignien des Fallschirmjägers wie H2. Beachten Sie die Z-70B-Maschinenpistole sowie gewebte Beuteltaschen für Magazine.

LE RÉQUISITIONNAIRE, EL VERDUGO

Honoré de Balzac

Le réquisitionnaire

« Tantôt ils lui voyaient, par un phénomène de vision ou de locomotion, abolir l'espace dans ses deux modes de Temps et de Distance, dont l'un est intellectuel et l'autre physique. »

Hist. intell. de LOUIS LAMBERT.

À mon cher Albert Marchand de la Ribellerie.

Tours, 1836.

Par un soir du mois de novembre 1793, les principaux personnages de Carentan se trouvaient dans le salon de madame de Dey, chez laquelle l'*assemblée* se tenait tous les jours. Quelques circonstances qui n'eussent point attiré l'attention d'une grande ville, mais qui devaient fortement en préoccuper une petite, prêtaient à ce rendez-vous habituel un intérêt inaccoutumé. La surveille, madame de Dey avait fermé sa porte à sa société, qu'elle s'était encore dispensée de recevoir la veille, en prétextant d'une indisposition. En temps ordinaire, ces deux événements eussent fait à Carentan le même effet que produit à Paris un *relâche* à tous les théâtres. Ces jours-là, l'existence est en quelque sorte incomplète. Mais, en 1793, la conduite de madame de Dey pouvait avoir les plus funestes résultats. La moindre démarche hasardée devenait alors presque toujours pour les nobles une question de vie ou de mort. Pour bien comprendre la curiosité vive et les étroites finesses qui animèrent pendant cette soirée les physionomies normandes de tous ces personnages, mais surtout pour partager les perplexités secrètes de madame de Dey, il est nécessaire d'expliquer le rôle qu'elle jouait à Carentan. La position critique dans laquelle elle se trouvait en ce moment ayant été sans doute celle de bien des gens pendant la Révolution, les sympathies de plus d'un lecteur achèveront de colorer ce récit.

Madame de Dey, veuve d'un lieutenant général, chevalier des

ordres, avait quitté la cour au commencement de l'émigration. Possédant des biens considérables aux environs de Carentan, elle s'y était réfugiée, en espérant que l'influence de la Terreur s'y ferait peu sentir. Ce calcul, fondé sur une connaissance exacte du pays, était juste. La Révolution exerça peu de ravages en Basse-Normandie. Quoique madame de Dey ne vît jadis que les familles nobles du pays quand elle y venait visiter ses propriétés, elle avait, par politique, ouvert sa maison aux principaux bourgeois de la ville et aux nouvelles autorités, en s'efforçant de les rendre fiers de sa conquête, sans réveiller chez eux ni haine ni jalousie. Gracieuse et bonne, douée de cette inexprimable douceur qui sait plaire sans recourir à l'abaissement ou à la prière, elle avait réussi à se concilier l'estime générale par un tact exquis dont les sages avertissements lui permettaient de se tenir sur la ligne délicate où elle pouvait satisfaire aux exigences de cette société mêlée, sans humilier le rétif amour-propre des parvenus, ni choquer celui de ses anciens amis.

Âgée d'environ trente-huit ans, elle conservait encore, non cette beauté fraîche et nourrie qui distingue les filles de la Basse-Normandie, mais une beauté grêle et pour ainsi dire aristocratique. Ses traits étaient fins et délicats ; sa taille était souple et déliée. Quand elle parlait, son pâle visage paraissait s'éclairer et prendre de la vie. Ses grands yeux noirs étaient pleins d'affabilité, mais leur expression calme et religieuse semblait annoncer que le principe de son existence n'était plus en elle. Mariée à la fleur de l'âge avec un militaire vieux et jaloux, la fausseté de sa position au milieu d'une cour galante contribua beaucoup sans doute à répandre un voile de grave mélancolie sur une figure où les charmes et la vivacité de l'amour avaient dû briller autrefois. Obligée de réprimer sans cesse les mouvements naïfs, les émotions de la femme alors qu'elle sent encore au lieu de réfléchir, la passion était restée vierge au fond de son cœur. Aussi, son principal attrait venait-il de cette intime jeunesse que, par moments, trahissait sa physionomie, et qui donnait à ses idées une innocente expression de désir. Son aspect commandait la retenue, mais il y avait toujours dans son maintien, dans sa voix, des élans vers un avenir inconnu, comme chez une jeune fille ; bientôt l'homme le plus insensible se trouvait amoureux d'elle, et conservait néanmoins une sorte de crainte respectueuse, inspirée par ses manières polies qui imposaient. Son âme, nativement grande, mais fortifiée par des luttes cruelles, semblait placée trop loin du vulgaire, et les hommes se faisaient justice. À cette âme, il fallait nécessairement une haute passion. Aussi les affections de madame de Dey s'étaient-elles concentrées dans un seul sentiment, celui de la maternité. Le bonheur et les plaisirs dont avait été privée sa vie de femme, elle les retrouvait dans l'amour extrême qu'elle portait à son fils. Elle ne l'aimait pas seulement avec le pur et profond dévouement d'une mère, mais avec la coquetterie d'une maîtresse, avec la jalousie d'une épouse. Elle était malheureuse loin de lui, inquiète pendant ses absences, ne le voyait jamais assez, ne vivait que par lui et pour lui. Afin de faire comprendre aux hommes la force de ce sentiment, il suffira d'ajouter que ce fils était non seulement l'unique enfant de madame de Dey, mais son dernier parent, le seul être auquel elle pût rattacher les craintes, les espérances et les joies de sa vie. Le feu comte de Dey fut le dernier rejeton de sa famille, comme elle se trouva seule héritière de la sienne. Les calculs et les intérêts humains s'étaient donc accordés avec les plus nobles besoins de l'âme pour exalter dans le cœur de la comtesse un sentiment déjà si fort chez les femmes. Elle n'avait élevé son fils qu'avec des peines infinies, qui le lui avaient rendu plus cher encore ; vingt fois les médecins lui en présagèrent la perte ; mais, confiante en ses pressentiments, en ses espérances, elle eut la joie inexprimable de lui voir heureusement traverser les périls de l'enfance, d'admirer les progrès de sa constitution, en dépit des arrêts de la Faculté.

Grâce à des soins constants, ce fils avait grandi et s'était si gracieusement développé, qu'à vingt ans, il passait pour un des cavaliers les plus accomplis de Versailles. Enfin, par un bonheur qui ne couronne pas les efforts de toutes les mères, elle était adorée de son fils ; leurs âmes s'entendaient par de fraternelles sympathies. S'ils n'eussent pas été liés déjà par le vœu de la nature, ils auraient instinctivement éprouvé l'un pour l'autre cette amitié d'homme à homme, si rare à rencontrer dans la vie. Nommé sous-lieutenant de dragons à dix-huit ans, le jeune comte avait obéi au point d'honneur de l'époque en suivant les princes dans leur émigration.

Ainsi madame de Dey, noble, riche, et mère d'un émigré, ne se dissimulait point les dangers de sa cruelle situation. Ne formant d'autre vœu que celui de conserver à son fils une grande fortune, elle avait renoncé au bonheur de l'accompagner ; mais en lisant les lois rigoureuses en vertu desquelles la République confisquait chaque jour les biens des émigrés à Carentan, elle s'applaudissait de cet acte de courage. Ne gardait-elle pas les trésors de son fils au péril de ses jours ? Puis, en apprenant les terribles exécutions ordonnées par la Convention, elle s'endormait heureuse de savoir sa seule richesse en sûreté, loin des dangers, loin des échafauds. Elle se complaisait à croire qu'elle avait pris le meilleur parti pour sauver à la fois toutes ses fortunes. Faisant à cette secrète pensée les concessions voulues par le malheur des temps, sans compromettre ni sa dignité de femme ni ses croyances aristocratiques, elle enveloppait ses douleurs dans un froid mystère. Elle avait compris les difficultés qui l'attendaient à Carentan. Venir y occuper la première place, n'était-ce pas y défier l'échafaud tous les jours ? Mais, soutenue par un courage de mère, elle sut conquérir l'affection des pauvres en soulageant indifféremment toutes les misères, et se rendit nécessaire aux riches en veillant à leurs plaisirs. Elle recevait le procureur de la commune, le maire, le président du district, l'accusateur public, et même les juges du tribunal révolutionnaire. Les quatre premiers de ces personnages, n'étant pas mariés, la courtisaient dans l'espoir de l'épouser, soit en l'effrayant par le mal qu'ils pouvaient lui faire, soit en lui offrant leur protection. L'accusateur public, ancien procureur à Caen, jadis chargé des intérêts de la comtesse, tentait de lui inspirer de l'amour par une conduite pleine de dévouement et de générosité ; finesse dangereuse ! Il était le plus redoutable de tous les prétendants. Lui seul connaissait à fond l'état de la fortune considérable de son ancienne cliente. Sa passion devait s'accroître de tous les désirs d'une avarice qui s'appuyait sur un pouvoir immense, sur le droit de vie et de mort dans le district. Cet homme, encore jeune, mettait tant de noblesse dans ses procédés, que madame de Dey n'avait pas encore pu le juger. Mais, méprisant le danger qu'il y avait à lutter d'adresse avec des Normands, elle employait l'esprit inventif et la ruse que la nature a départis aux femmes pour opposer ces rivalités les unes aux autres. En gagnant du temps, elle espérait arriver saine et sauve à la fin des troubles. À cette époque, les royalistes de l'intérieur se flattaient tous les jours de voir la Révolution terminée le lendemain ; et cette conviction a été la perte de beaucoup d'entre eux.

Malgré ces obstacles, la comtesse avait assez habilement maintenu son indépendance jusqu'au jour où, par une inexplicable imprudence, elle s'était avisée de fermer sa porte. Elle inspirait un intérêt si profond et si véritable, que les personnes venues ce soir-là chez elle conçurent de vives inquiétudes en apprenant qu'il lui devenait impossible de les recevoir ; puis, avec cette franchise de curiosité empreinte dans les mœurs provinciales, elles s'enquirent du malheur, du chagrin, de la maladie qui devait affliger madame de Dey. À ces questions une vieille femme de charge, nommée Brigitte, répondait que sa maîtresse s'était enfermée et ne voulait voir personne, pas même les gens de sa maison. L'existence, en quelque sorte claustrale, que mènent les habitants d'une petite ville crée en eux une habitude d'analyser et d'expliquer les actions d'autrui si naturellement invincible qu'après avoir plaint madame de Dey, sans savoir si elle était réellement heureuse ou chagrine, chacun se mit à rechercher les causes de sa soudaine retraite.

– Si elle était malade, dit le premier curieux, elle aurait envoyé chez le médecin ; mais le docteur est resté pendant toute la journée chez moi à jouer aux échecs ! Il me disait en riant que, par le temps qui court, il n'y a qu'une maladie... et qu'elle est malheureusement incurable.

Cette plaisanterie fut prudemment hasardée. Femmes, hommes, vieillards et jeunes filles se mirent alors à parcourir le vaste champ des conjectures. Chacun crut entrevoir un secret, et ce secret occupa toutes les imaginations. Le lendemain les soupçons s'envenimèrent. Comme la vie est à jour dans une petite ville, les femmes apprirent les premières que Brigitte avait fait au marché des provisions plus considérables qu'à l'ordinaire. Ce fait ne pouvait être contesté. L'on avait vu Brigitte de grand matin sur la place, et, chose extraordinaire, elle y avait acheté le seul lièvre qui s'y trouvât. Toute la ville savait que madame de Dey n'aimait pas le gibier. Le lièvre devint un point de départ pour des suppositions infinies. En faisant leur promenade périodique, les vieillards remarquèrent dans la maison de la comtesse, une sorte d'activité concentrée qui se révélait par les précautions même dont se servaient les gens pour la cacher. Le valet de chambre battait un tapis dans le jardin ; la veille, personne n'y aurait pris garde ; mais ce tapis devint une pièce à l'appui des romans que tout le monde bâtissait. Chacun avait le sien. Le second jour, en apprenant que madame de Dey se disait indisposée, les principaux personnages de Carentan se réunirent le soir chez le frère du maire, vieux négociant marié, homme probe, généralement estimé, et pour lequel la comtesse avait beaucoup d'égards. Là, tous les aspirants à la main de la riche veuve eurent à raconter une fable plus ou moins probable ; et chacun d'eux pensait à faire tourner à son profit la circonstance secrète qui la forçait de se compromettre ainsi. L'accusateur public imaginait tout un drame pour amener nuitamment le fils de madame de Dey chez elle. Le maire croyait à un prêtre insermenté, venu de la Vendée, et qui lui aurait demandé un asile ; mais l'achat du lièvre, un vendredi, l'embarrassait beaucoup. Le président du district tenait fortement pour un chef de Chouans ou de Vendéens vivement poursuivi. D'autres voulaient un noble échappé des prisons de Paris. Enfin tous soupçonnaient la comtesse d'être coupable d'une de ces générosités que les lois d'alors nommaient un crime, et qui pouvaient conduire à l'échafaud. L'accusateur public disait d'ailleurs à voix basse qu'il fallait se taire, et tâcher de sauver l'infortunée de l'abîme vers lequel elle marchait à grands pas.

– Si vous ébruitez cette affaire, ajouta-t-il, je serai obligé d'intervenir, de faire des perquisitions chez elle, et alors !... Il n'acheva pas, mais chacun comprit cette réticence.

Les amis sincères de la comtesse s'alarmèrent tellement pour elle que, dans la matinée du troisième jour, le procureur-syndic de la commune lui fit écrire par sa femme un mot pour l'engager à recevoir pendant la soirée comme à l'ordinaire. Plus hardi, le vieux négociant se présenta dans la matinée chez madame de Dey. Fort du service qu'il voulait lui rendre, il exigea d'être introduit auprès d'elle, et resta stupéfait en l'apercevant dans le jardin, occupée à couper les dernières fleurs de ses plates-bandes pour en garnir des vases.

– Elle a sans doute donné asile à son amant, se dit le vieillard pris de pitié pour cette charmante femme. La singulière expression du visage de la comtesse le confirma dans ses soupçons. Vivement ému de ce dévouement si naturel aux femmes, mais qui nous touche toujours, parce que tous les hommes sont flattés par les sacrifices qu'une d'elles fait à un homme, le négociant instruisit la comtesse des bruits qui couraient dans la ville et du danger où elle se trouvait. – Car, lui dit-il en terminant, si, parmi nos fonctionnaires, il en est quelques-uns assez disposés à vous pardonner un héroïsme qui aurait un prêtre pour objet, personne ne vous plaindra si l'on vient à découvrir que vous vous immolez à des intérêts de cœur.

À ces mots, madame de Dey regarda le vieillard avec un air d'égarement et de folie qui le fit frissonner, lui, vieillard.

– Venez, lui dit-elle en le prenant par la main pour le conduire dans sa chambre, où, après s'être assurée qu'ils étaient seuls, elle tira de son sein une lettre sale et chiffonnée : – Lisez, s'écria-t-elle en faisant un violent effort pour prononcer ce mot.

Elle tomba dans son fauteuil, comme anéantie. Pendant que le vieux négociant cherchait ses lunettes et les nettoyait, elle leva les yeux sur lui, le contempla pour la première fois avec curiosité ; puis, d'une voix altérée : – Je me fie à vous, lui dit-elle doucement.

– Est-ce que je ne viens pas partager votre crime ? répondit le bonhomme avec simplicité.

Elle tressaillit. Pour la première fois, dans cette petite ville, son âme sympathisait avec celle d'un autre. Le vieux négociant comprit tout à coup et l'abattement et la joie de la comtesse. Son fils avait fait partie de l'expédition de Granville, il écrivait à sa mère du fond de sa prison, en lui donnant un triste et doux espoir. Ne doutant pas de ses moyens d'évasion, il lui indiquait trois jours pendant lesquels il devait se présenter chez elle, déguisé. La fatale lettre contenait de déchirants adieux au cas où il ne serait pas à Carentan dans la soirée du troisième jour, et il priait sa mère de remettre une assez forte somme à l'émissaire qui s'était chargé de lui apporter cette dépêche, à travers mille dangers. Le papier tremblait dans les mains du vieillard.

– Et voici le troisième jour, s'écria madame de Dey qui se leva rapidement, reprit la lettre, et marcha.

– Vous avez commis des imprudences, lui dit le négociant. Pourquoi faire prendre des provisions ?

– Mais il peut arriver, mourant de faim, exténué de fatigue, et... Elle n'acheva pas.

– Je suis sûr de mon frère, reprit le vieillard, je vais aller le mettre dans vos intérêts.

Le négociant retrouva dans cette circonstance la finesse qu'il avait mise jadis dans les affaires, et lui dicta des conseils empreints de prudence et de sagacité. Après être convenus de tout ce qu'ils devaient dire et faire l'un ou l'autre, le vieillard alla, sous des prétextes habilement trouvés, dans les principales maisons de

Carentan, où il annonça que madame de Dey, qu'il venait de voir, recevrait dans la soirée, malgré son indisposition. Luttant de finesse avec les intelligences normandes dans l'interrogatoire que chaque famille lui imposa sur la nature de la maladie de la comtesse, il réussit à donner le change à presque toutes les personnes qui s'occupaient de cette mystérieuse affaire. Sa première visite fit merveille. Il raconta devant une vieille dame goutteuse que madame de Dey avait manqué périr d'une attaque de goutte à l'estomac ; le fameux Tronchin lui ayant recommandé jadis, en pareille occurrence, de se mettre sur la poitrine la peau d'un lièvre écorché vif, et de rester au lit sans se permettre le moindre mouvement, la comtesse, en danger de mort, il y a deux jours, se trouvait, après avoir suivi ponctuellement la bizarre ordonnance de Tronchin, assez bien rétablie pour recevoir ceux qui viendraient la voir pendant la soirée. Ce conte eut un succès prodigieux, et le médecin de Carentan, royaliste *in petto*, en augmenta l'effet par l'importance avec laquelle il discuta le spécifique. Néanmoins les soupçons avaient trop fortement pris racine dans l'esprit de quelques entêtés ou de quelques philosophes pour être entièrement dissipés ; en sorte que, le soir, ceux qui étaient admis chez madame de Dey vinrent avec empressement et de bonne heure chez elle, les uns pour épier sa contenance, les autres par amitié, la plupart saisis par le merveilleux de sa guérison. Ils trouvèrent la comtesse assise au coin de la grande cheminée de son salon, à peu près aussi modeste que l'étaient ceux de Carentan ; car, pour ne pas blesser les étroites pensées de ses hôtes, elle s'était refusée aux jouissances de luxe auxquelles elle était jadis habituée, elle n'avait donc rien changé chez elle. Le carreau de la salle de réception n'était même pas frotté. Elle laissait sur les murs de vieilles tapisseries sombres, conservait les meubles du pays, brûlait de la chandelle, et suivait les modes de la ville, en épousant la vie provinciale sans reculer ni devant les petitesses les plus dures, ni devant les privations les plus désagréables. Mais sachant que ses hôtes lui pardonneraient les magnificences qui auraient leur bien-être pour but, elle ne négligeait rien quand il s'agissait de leur procurer des jouissances personnelles. Aussi leur donnait-elle d'excellents dîners. Elle allait jusqu'à feindre de l'avarice pour plaire à ces esprits calculateurs ; et, après avoir eu l'art de se faire arracher certaines concessions de luxe, elle savait obéir avec grâce. Donc, vers sept heures du soir, la meilleure mauvaise compagnie de Carentan se trouvait chez elle, et décrivait un grand cercle devant la cheminée. La maîtresse du logis, soutenue dans son malheur par les regards compatissants que lui jetait le vieux négociant, se soumit avec un courage inouï aux questions minutieuses, aux raisonnements frivoles et stupides de ses hôtes. Mais à chaque coup de marteau frappé sur sa porte, ou toutes les fois que des pas retentissaient dans la rue, elle cachait ses émotions en soulevant des questions intéressantes pour la fortune du pays. Elle éleva de bruyantes discussions sur la qualité des cidres, et fut si bien secondée par son confident, que l'assemblée oublia presque de l'espionner en trouvant sa contenance naturelle et son aplomb imperturbable. L'accusateur public et l'un des juges du tribunal révolutionnaire restaient taciturnes, observaient avec attention les moindres mouvements de sa physionomie, écoutaient dans la maison, malgré le tumulte ; et, à plusieurs reprises, ils lui firent des questions embarrassantes, auxquelles la comtesse répondit cependant avec une admirable présence d'esprit. Les mères ont tant de courage ! Au moment où madame de Dey eut arrangé les parties, placé tout le monde à des tables de boston, de reversis ou de whist, elle resta encore à causer auprès de quelques jeunes personnes avec un extrême laisser-aller, en jouant son rôle en actrice consommée. Elle se fit demander un loto, prétendit savoir seule où il était, et disparut.

– J'étouffe, ma pauvre Brigitte, s'écria-t-elle en essuyant des larmes qui sortirent vivement de ses yeux brillants de fièvre, de douleur et d'impatience. – Il ne vient pas, reprit-elle en regardant la chambre où elle était montée. Ici, je respire et je vis. Encore quelques moments, et il sera là, pourtant ! car il vit encore, j'en suis certaine. Mon cœur me le dit. N'entendez-vous rien, Brigitte ? Oh ! je donnerais le reste de ma vie pour savoir s'il est en prison ou s'il marche à travers la campagne ! Je voudrais ne pas penser.

Elle examina de nouveau si tout était en ordre dans l'appartement. Un bon feu brillait dans la cheminée ; les volets étaient soigneusement fermés ; les meubles reluisaient de propreté ; la manière dont avait été fait le lit, prouvait que la comtesse s'était occupée avec Brigitte des moindres détails ; et ses espérances se trahissaient dans les soins délicats qui paraissaient avoir été pris dans cette chambre où se respiraient et la gracieuse douceur de l'amour et ses plus chastes caresses dans les parfums exhalés par les fleurs. Une mère seule pouvait avoir prévu les désirs d'un soldat et lui préparer de si complètes satisfactions. Un repas exquis, des vins choisis, la chaussure, le linge, enfin tout ce qui devait être nécessaire ou agréable à un voyageur fatigué, se trouvait rassemblé pour que rien ne lui manquât, pour que les délices du chez-soi lui révélassent l'amour d'une mère.

– Brigitte ? dit la comtesse d'un son de voix déchirant en allant placer un siège devant la table, comme pour donner de la réalité à ses vœux, comme pour augmenter la force de ses illusions.

– Ah ! madame, il viendra. Il n'est pas loin. – Je ne doute pas qu'il ne vive et qu'il ne soit en marche, reprit Brigitte. J'ai mis une clef dans la Bible, et je l'ai tenue sur mes doigts pendant que Cottin lisait l'Évangile de saint Jean... et, madame ! la clef n'a pas tourné.

– Est-ce bien sûr ? demanda la comtesse.

– Oh ! madame, c'est connu. Je gagerais mon salut qu'il vit encore. Dieu ne peut pas se tromper.

– Malgré le danger qui l'attend ici, je voudrais bien cependant l'y voir...

– Pauvre monsieur Auguste, s'écria Brigitte, il est sans doute à pied, par les chemins.

– Et voilà huit heures qui sonnent au clocher, s'écria la comtesse avec terreur.

Elle eut peur d'être restée plus longtemps qu'elle ne le devait, dans cette chambre où elle croyait à la vie de son fils, en voyant tout ce qui lui en attestait la vie, elle descendit ; mais avant d'entrer au salon, elle resta pendant un moment sous le péristyle de l'escalier, en écoutant si quelque bruit ne réveillait pas les silencieux échos de la ville. Elle sourit au mari de Brigitte, qui se tenait en sentinelle, et dont les yeux semblaient hébétés à force de prêter attention aux murmures de la place et de la nuit. Elle voyait son fils en tout et partout. Elle rentra bientôt, en affectant un air gai, et se mit à jouer au loto avec des petites filles ; mais, de temps en temps, elle se plaignit de souffrir, et revint occuper son fauteuil auprès de la cheminée.

Telle était la situation des choses et des esprits dans la maison de madame de Dey, pendant que, sur le chemin de Paris à Cherbourg, un jeune homme vêtu d'une carmagnole brune, costume de rigueur à cette époque, se dirigeait vers Carentan. À l'origine des

11/26

réquisitions, il y avait peu ou point de discipline. Les exigences du moment ne permettaient guère à la République d'équiper sur-le-champ ses soldats, et il n'était pas rare de voir les chemins couverts de réquisitionnaires qui conservaient leurs habits bourgeois. Ces jeunes gens devançaient leurs bataillons aux lieux d'étape, ou restaient en arrière, car leur marche était soumise à leur manière de supporter les fatigues d'une longue route. Le voyageur dont il est ici question se trouvait assez en avant de la colonne de réquisitionnaires qui se rendait à Cherbourg, et que le maire de Carentan attendait d'heure en heure, afin de leur distribuer des billets de logement. Ce jeune homme marchait d'un pas alourdi, mais ferme encore, et son allure semblait annoncer qu'il s'était familiarisé depuis longtemps avec les rudesses de la vie militaire. Quoique la lune éclairât les herbages qui avoisinent Carentan, il avait remarqué de gros nuages blancs prêts à jeter de la neige sur la campagne ; et la crainte d'être surpris par un ouragan animait sans doute sa démarche, alors plus vive que ne le comportait sa lassitude. Il avait sur le dos un sac presque vide, et tenait à la main une canne de buis, coupée dans les hautes et larges haies que cet arbuste forme autour de la plupart des herbages en Basse-Normandie. Ce voyageur solitaire entra dans Carentan, dont les tours, bordées de lueurs fantastiques par la lune, lui apparaissaient depuis un moment. Son pas réveilla les échos des rues silencieuses, où il ne rencontra personne ; il fut obligé de demander la maison du maire à un tisserand qui travaillait encore. Ce magistrat demeurait à une faible distance, et le réquisitionnaire se vit bientôt à l'abri sous le porche de la maison du maire, et s'y assit sur un banc de pierre, en attendant le billet de logement qu'il avait réclamé. Mais mandé par ce fonctionnaire, il comparut devant lui, et devint l'objet d'un scrupuleux examen. Le fantassin était un jeune homme de bonne mine qui paraissait appartenir à une famille distinguée. Son air trahissait la noblesse. L'intelligence due à une bonne éducation respirait sur sa figure.

– Comment te nommes-tu ? lui demanda le maire en lui jetant un regard plein de finesse.

– Julien Jussieu, répondit le réquisitionnaire.

– Et tu viens ? dit le magistrat en laissant échapper un sourire d'incrédulité.

– De Paris.

– Tes camarades doivent être loin, reprit le Normand d'un ton railleur.

– J'ai trois lieues d'avance sur le bataillon.

– Quelque sentiment t'attire sans doute à Carentan, citoyen réquisitionnaire ? dit le maire d'un air fin. C'est bien, ajouta-t-il en imposant silence par un geste de main au jeune homme prêt à parler, nous savons où t'envoyer. Tiens, ajouta-t-il en lui remettant son billet de logement, va, *citoyen Jussieu !*

Un teinte d'ironie se fit sentir dans l'accent avec lequel le magistrat prononça ces deux derniers mots, en tendant un billet sur lequel la demeure de madame de Dey était indiquée. Le jeune homme lut l'adresse avec un air de curiosité.

– Il sait bien qu'il n'a pas loin à aller. Et quand il sera dehors, il aura bientôt traversé la place ! s'écria le maire en se parlant à lui-même pendant que le jeune homme sortait. Il est joliment hardi ! Que Dieu le conduise ! Il a réponse à tout. Oui, mais si un autre que moi lui avait demandé à voir ses papiers, il était perdu !

En ce moment, les horloges de Carentan avaient sonné neuf heures et demie ; les falots s'allumaient dans l'antichambre de madame de Dey ; les domestiques aidaient leurs maîtresses et leurs maîtres à mettre leurs sabots, leurs houppelandes ou leurs mantelets ; les joueurs avaient soldé leurs comptes, et allaient se retirer tous ensemble, suivant l'usage établi dans toutes les petites villes.

– Il paraît que l'accusateur veut rester, dit une dame en s'apercevant que ce personnage important leur manquait au moment où chacun se sépara sur la place pour regagner son logis, après avoir épuisé toutes les formules d'adieu.

Ce terrible magistrat était en effet seul avec la comtesse, qui attendait, en tremblant, qu'il lui plût de sortir.

– Citoyenne, dit-il enfin après un long silence qui eut quelque chose d'effrayant, je suis ici pour faire observer les lois de la République...

Madame de Dey frissonna.

– N'as-tu donc rien à me révéler ? demanda-t-il.

– Rien, répondit-elle étonnée.

– Ah ! madame, s'écria l'accusateur en s'asseyant auprès d'elle et changeant de ton, en ce moment, faute d'un mot, vous ou moi, nous pouvons porter notre tête sur l'échafaud. J'ai trop bien observé votre caractère, votre âme, vos manières, pour partager l'erreur dans laquelle vous avez su mettre votre société ce soir. Vous attendez votre fils, je n'en saurais douter.

La comtesse laissa échapper un geste de dénégation ; mais elle avait pâli, mais les muscles de son visage s'étaient contractés par la nécessité où elle se trouvait d'afficher une fermeté trompeuse, et l'œil implacable de l'accusateur public ne perdit aucun de ses mouvements.

– Eh ! bien, recevez-le, reprit le magistrat révolutionnaire ; mais qu'il ne reste pas plus tard que sept heures du matin sous votre toit. Demain, au jour, armé d'une dénonciation que je me ferai faire, je viendrai chez vous...

Elle le regarda d'un air stupide qui aurait fait pitié à un tigre.

– Je démontrerai, poursuivit-il d'une voix douce, la fausseté de la dénonciation par d'exactes perquisitions, et vous serez, par la nature de mon rapport, à l'abri de tous soupçons ultérieurs. Je parlerai de vos dons patriotiques, de votre civisme, et nous serons *tous* sauvés.

Madame de Dey craignait un piège, elle restait immobile, mais son visage était en feu et sa langue glacée. Un coup de marteau retentit dans la maison.

– Ah ! cria la mère épouvantée, en tombant à genoux. Le sauver, le sauver !

– Oui, sauvons-le ! reprit l'accusateur public, en lui lançant un regard de passion, dût-il *nous* en coûter la vie.

– Je suis perdue, s'écria-t-elle pendant que l'accusateur la relevait avec politesse.

– Eh ! madame, répondit-il par un beau mouvement oratoire, je ne veux vous devoir à rien... qu'à vous-même.

– Madame, le voi..., s'écria Brigitte qui croyait sa maîtresse seule.

À l'aspect de l'accusateur public, la vieille servante, de rouge et joyeuse qu'elle était, devint immobile et blême.

– Qui est-ce, Brigitte ? demanda le magistrat d'un air doux et intelligent.

– Un réquisitionnaire que le maire nous envoie à loger, répondit la servante en montrant le billet.

– C'est vrai, dit l'accusateur après avoir lu le papier. Il nous arrive un bataillon ce soir !

Et il sortit.

La comtesse avait trop besoin de croire en ce moment à la sincérité de son ancien procureur pour concevoir le moindre doute ; elle monta rapidement l'escalier, ayant à peine la force de se soutenir ; puis, elle ouvrit la porte de sa chambre, vit son fils, se précipita dans ses bras, mourante : – Oh ! mon enfant, mon enfant ! s'écria-t-elle en sanglotant et le couvrant de baisers empreints d'une sorte de frénésie.

– Madame, dit l'inconnu.

– Ah ! ce n'est pas lui, cria-t-elle en reculant d'épouvante et restant debout devant le réquisitionnaire qu'elle contemplait d'un air hagard.

– Ô saint bon Dieu, quelle ressemblance ! dit Brigitte.

Il y eut un moment de silence, et l'étranger lui-même tressaillit à l'aspect de madame de Dey.

– Ah ! monsieur, dit-elle en s'appuyant sur le mari de Brigitte, et sentant alors dans toute son étendue une douleur dont la première atteinte avait failli la tuer ; monsieur, je ne saurais vous voir plus longtemps, souffrez que mes gens me remplacent et s'occupent de vous.

Elle descendit chez elle, à demi portée par Brigitte et son vieux serviteur.

– Comment, madame ! s'écria la femme de charge en asseyant sa maîtresse, cet homme va-t-il coucher dans le lit de monsieur Auguste, mettre les pantoufles de monsieur Auguste, manger le pâté que j'ai fait pour monsieur Auguste ! quand on devrait me guillotiner, je...

– Brigitte ! cria madame de Dey.

Brigitte resta muette.

– Tais-toi donc, bavarde, lui dit son mari à voix basse, veux-tu tuer madame ?

En ce moment, le réquisitionnaire fit du bruit dans sa chambre en se mettant à table.

– Je ne resterai pas ici, s'écria madame de Dey, j'irai dans la serre, d'où j'entendrai mieux ce qui se passera au dehors pendant la nuit.

Elle flottait encore entre la crainte d'avoir perdu son fils et l'espérance de le voir reparaître. La nuit fut horriblement silencieuse. Il y eut, pour la comtesse, un moment affreux, quand le bataillon des réquisitionnaires vint en ville et que chaque homme y chercha son logement. Ce fut des espérances trompées à chaque pas, à chaque bruit ; puis bientôt la nature reprit un calme effrayant. Vers le matin, la comtesse fut obligée de rentrer chez elle. Brigitte, qui surveillait les mouvements de sa maîtresse, ne la voyant pas sortir, entra dans la chambre et y trouva la comtesse morte.

– Elle aura probablement entendu ce réquisitionnaire qui achève de s'habiller et qui marche dans la chambre de monsieur Auguste en chantant leur damnée *Marseillaise*, comme s'il était dans une écurie, s'écria Brigitte. Ça l'aura tuée !

La mort de la comtesse fut causée par un sentiment plus grave, et sans doute par quelque vision terrible. À l'heure précise où madame de Dey mourait à Carentan, son fils était fusillé dans le Morbihan. Nous pouvons joindre ce fait tragique à toutes les observations sur les sympathies qui méconnaissent les lois de l'espace ; documents que rassemblent avec une savante curiosité quelques hommes de solitude, et qui serviront un jour à asseoir les bases d'une science nouvelle à laquelle il a manqué jusqu'à ce jour un homme de génie.

Paris, février 1831.

El Verdugo

À Martinez de la Rosa.

Le clocher de la petite ville de Menda venait de sonner minuit. En ce moment, un jeune officier français, appuyé sur le parapet d'une longue terrasse qui bordait les jardins du château de Menda, paraissait abîmé dans une contemplation plus profonde que ne le comportait l'insouciance de la vie militaire ; mais il faut dire aussi que jamais heure, site et nuit ne furent plus propices à la méditation. Le beau ciel d'Espagne étendait un dôme d'azur au-dessus de sa tête. Le scintillement des étoiles et la douce lumière de la lune éclairaient une vallée délicieuse qui se déroulait coquettement à ses pieds. Appuyé sur un oranger en fleur, le chef de bataillon pouvait voir, à cent pieds au-dessous de lui, la ville de Menda, qui semblait s'être mise à l'abri des vents du nord, au pied du rocher sur lequel était bâti le château. En tournant la tête, il apercevait la mer, dont les eaux brillantes encadraient le paysage d'une large lame d'argent. Le château était illuminé. Le joyeux tumulte d'un bal, les accents de l'orchestre, les rires de quelques officiers et de leurs danseuses arrivaient jusqu'à lui, mêlés au lointain murmure des flots. La fraîcheur de la nuit imprimait une sorte d'énergie à son corps fatigué par la chaleur du jour. Enfin les jardins étaient plantés d'arbres si odoriférants et de fleurs si suaves, que le jeune homme se trouvait comme plongé dans un bain de parfums.

Le château de Menda appartenait à un grand d'Espagne, qui l'habitait en ce moment avec sa famille. Pendant toute cette soirée, l'aînée des filles avait regardé l'officier avec un intérêt empreint d'une telle tristesse, que le sentiment de compassion exprimé par l'Espagnole pouvait bien causer la rêverie du Français. Clara était belle, et quoiqu'elle eût trois frères et une soeur, les biens du marquis de Léganès paraissaient assez considérables pour faire croire à Victor Marchand que la jeune personne aurait une riche dot. Mais comment oser croire que la fille du vieillard le plus entiché de sa grandesse qui fût en Espagne, pourrait être donnée au fils d'un épicier de Paris ! D'ailleurs, les Français étaient haïs. Le marquis ayant été soupçonné par le général G..t..r, qui gouvernait la province, de préparer un soulèvement en faveur de Ferdinand VII, le bataillon commandé par Victor Marchand avait été cantonné dans la petite ville de Menda pour contenir les campagnes voisines, qui obéissaient au marquis de Léganès. Une récente dépêche du maréchal Ney faisait craindre que les Anglais ne débarquassent prochainement sur la côte, et signalait le marquis comme un homme qui entretenait des intelligences avec le cabinet de Londres. Aussi, malgré le bon accueil que cet Espagnol avait fait à Victor Marchand et à ses soldats, le jeune officier se tenait-il constamment sur ses gardes. En se dirigeant vers cette terrasse où il venait examiner l'état de la ville et des campagnes confiées à sa surveillance, il se demandait comment il devait interpréter l'amitié que le marquis n'avait cessé de lui témoigner, et comment la tranquillité du pays pouvait se concilier avec les inquiétudes de son général ; mais depuis un moment, ces pensées avaient été chassées de l'esprit du jeune commandant par un sentiment de prudence et par une curiosité bien légitime. Il venait d'apercevoir dans la ville une assez grande quantité de lumières. Malgré la fête de saint Jacques, il avait ordonné, le matin même, que les feux fussent éteints à l'heure prescrite par son règlement. Le château seul avait été excepté de cette mesure. Il vit bien briller çà et là les baïonnettes de ses soldats aux postes accoutumés ; mais le silence était solennel, et rien n'annonçait que les Espagnols fussent en proie à l'ivresse d'une fête. Après avoir cherché à s'expliquer l'infraction dont se rendaient coupables les habitants, il trouva dans ce délit un mystère d'autant plus incompréhensible qu'il avait laissé des officiers chargés de la police nocturne et des rondes. Avec l'impétuosité de la jeunesse, il allait s'élancer par une brèche pour descendre rapidement les rochers, et parvenir ainsi plus tôt que par le chemin ordinaire à un petit poste placé à l'entrée de la ville du côté du château, quand un faible bruit l'arrêta dans sa course. Il crut entendre le sable des allées criant sous le pas léger d'une femme. Il retourna la tête et ne vit rien ; mais ses yeux furent saisis par l'éclat extraordinaire de l'Océan. Il y aperçut tout à coup un spectacle si funeste, qu'il demeura immobile de surprise, en accusant ses sens d'erreur. Les rayons blanchissants de la lune lui permirent de distinguer des voiles à une assez grande distance. Il tressaillit, et tâcha de se convaincre que cette vision était un piège d'optique offert par les fantaisies des ondes et de la lune. En ce moment, une voix enrouée prononça le nom de l'officier, qui regarda vers la brèche, et vit s'y élever lentement la tête du soldat par lequel il s'était fait accompagner au château.

– Est-ce vous, mon commandant ?

– Oui. Eh ! bien ? lui dit à voix basse le jeune homme, qu'une sorte de pressentiment avertit d'agir avec mystère.

– Ces gredins-là se remuent comme des vers, et je me hâte, si vous le permettez, de vous communiquer mes petites observations.

– Parle, répondit Victor Marchand.

– Je viens de suivre un homme du château qui s'est dirigé par ici une lanterne à la main. Une lanterne est furieusement suspecte ! je ne crois pas que ce chrétien-là ait besoin d'allumer des cierges à cette heure-ci. Ils veulent nous manger ! que je me suis dit, et je me suis mis à lui examiner les talons. Aussi, mon commandant, ai-je découvert à trois pas d'ici, sur un quartier de roche, un certain amas de fagots.

Un cri terrible qui tout à coup retentit dans la ville, interrompit le soldat. Une lueur soudaine éclaira le commandant. Le pauvre grenadier reçut une balle dans la tête et tomba. Un feu de paille et de bois sec brillait comme un incendie à dix pas du jeune homme. Les instruments et les rires cessaient de se faire entendre dans la salle du bal. Un silence de mort, interrompu par des gémissements, avait soudain remplacé les rumeurs et la musique de la fête. Un coup de canon retentit sur la plaine blanche de l'Océan. Une sueur froide coula sur le front du jeune officier. Il était sans épée. Il comprenait que ses soldats avaient péri et que les Anglais allaient débarquer. Il se vit déshonoré s'il vivait, il se vit traduit devant un conseil de guerre ; alors il mesura des yeux la profondeur de la vallée, et s'y élançait au moment où la main de Clara saisit la sienne.

– Fuyez ! dit-elle, mes frères me suivent pour vous tuer. Au bas du rocher, par là, vous trouverez l'andalou de Juanito. Allez !

Elle le poussa, le jeune homme stupéfait la regarda pendant un moment ; mais, obéissant bientôt à l'instinct de conservation qui n'abandonne jamais l'homme, même le plus fort, il s'élança dans le parc en prenant la direction indiquée, et courut à travers des rochers que les chèvres avaient seules pratiqués jusqu'alors. Il entendit Clara crier à ses frères de le poursuivre ; il entendit les pas de ses assassins ; il entendit siffler à ses oreilles les balles de plusieurs décharges ; mais il atteignit la vallée, trouva le cheval, monta dessus et disparut avec la rapidité de l'éclair.

En peu d'heures le jeune officier parvint au quartier du général G..t..r, qu'il trouva dînant avec son état-major.

– Je vous apporte ma tête ! s'écria le chef de bataillon en apparaissant pâle et défait.

Il s'assit, et raconta l'horrible aventure. Un silence effrayant accueillit son récit.

– Je vous trouve plus malheureux que criminel, répondit enfin le terrible général. Vous n'êtes pas comptable du forfait des Espagnols ; et à moins que le maréchal n'en décide autrement, je vous absous.

Ces paroles ne donnèrent qu'une bien faible consolation au malheureux officier.

– Quand l'empereur saura cela ! s'écria-t-il.

– Il voudra vous faire fusiller, dit le général, mais nous verrons. Enfin, ne parlons plus de ceci, ajouta-t-il d'un ton sévère, que pour en tirer une vengeance qui imprime une terreur salutaire à ce pays où l'on fait la guerre à la façon des Sauvages.

Une heure après, un régiment entier, un détachement de cavalerie et un convoi d'artillerie étaient en route. Le général et Victor marchaient à la tête de cette colonne. Les soldats, instruits du massacre de leurs camarades, étaient possédés d'une fureur sans exemple. La distance qui séparait la ville de Menda du quartier général fut franchie avec une rapidité miraculeuse. Sur la route, le général trouva des villages entiers sous les armes. Chacune de ces misérables bourgades fut cernée et leurs habitants décimés.

Par une de ces fatalités inexplicables, les vaisseaux anglais étaient restés en panne sans avancer ; mais on sut plus tard que ces vaisseaux ne portaient que de l'artillerie et qu'ils avaient mieux marché que le reste des transports. Ainsi la ville de Menda, privée des défenseurs qu'elle attendait, et que l'apparition des voiles anglaises semblait lui promettre, fut entourée par les troupes françaises presque sans coup férir. Les habitants, saisis de terreur, offrirent de se rendre à discrétion. Par un de ces dévouements qui n'ont pas été rares dans la Péninsule, les assassins des Français, prévoyant, d'après la cruauté connue du général, que Menda serait peut-être livrée aux flammes et la population entière passée au fil de l'épée, proposèrent de se dénoncer eux-mêmes au général. Il accepta cette offre, en y mettant pour condition que les habitants du château, depuis le dernier valet jusqu'au marquis, seraient mis entre ses mains. Cette capitulation consentie, le général promit de faire grâce au reste de la population et d'empêcher ses soldats de piller la ville ou d'y mettre le feu. Une contribution énorme fut frappée, et les plus riches habitants se constituèrent prisonniers pour en garantir le paiement, qui devait être effectué dans les vingt-quatre heures.

Le général prit toutes les précautions nécessaires à la sûreté de ses troupes, pourvut à la défense du pays, et refusa de loger ses soldats dans les maisons. Après les avoir fait camper, il monta au château et s'en empara militairement. Les membres de la famille de Léganès et les domestiques furent soigneusement gardés à vue, garrottés, et enfermés dans la salle où le bal avait eu lieu. Des fenêtres de cette pièce on pouvait facilement embrasser la terrasse qui dominait la ville. L'état-major s'établit dans une galerie voisine, où le général tint d'abord conseil sur les mesures à prendre pour s'opposer au débarquement. Après avoir expédié un aide de camp au maréchal Ney, ordonné d'établir des batteries sur la côte, le général et son état-major s'occupèrent des prisonniers. Deux cents Espagnols que les habitants avaient livrés furent immédiatement fusillés sur la terrasse. Après cette exécution militaire, le général commanda de planter sur la terrasse autant de potences qu'il y avait de gens dans la salle du château et de faire venir le bourreau de la ville. Victor Marchand profita du temps qui allait s'écouler avant le dîner pour aller voir les prisonniers. Il revint bientôt vers le général.

– J'accours, lui dit-il d'une voix émue, vous demander des grâces.

– Vous ! reprit le général avec un ton d'ironie amère.

– Hélas ! répondit Victor, je demande de tristes grâces. Le marquis, en voyant planter les potences, a espéré que vous changeriez ce genre de supplice pour sa famille, et vous supplie de faire décapiter les nobles.

– Soit, dit le général.

– Ils demandent encore qu'on leur accorde les secours de la religion, et qu'on les délivre de leurs liens ; ils promettent de ne pas chercher à fuir.

– J'y consens, dit le général ; mais vous m'en répondez.

– Le vieillard vous offre encore toute sa fortune si vous voulez pardonner à son jeune fils.

– Vraiment ! répondit le chef. Ses biens appartiennent déjà au roi Joseph. Il s'arrêta. Une pensée de mépris rida son front, et il ajouta : – Je vais surpasser leur désir. Je devine l'importance de sa dernière demande. Eh ! bien, qu'il achète l'éternité de son nom, mais que l'Espagne se souvienne à jamais de sa trahison et de son supplice ! Je laisse sa fortune et la vie à celui de ses fils qui remplira l'office de bourreau. Allez, et ne m'en parlez plus.

Le dîner était servi. Les officiers attablés satisfaisaient un appétit que la fatigue avait aiguillonné. Un seul d'entre eux, Victor Marchand, manquait au festin. Après avoir hésité longtemps, il entra dans le salon où gémissait l'orgueilleuse famille de Léganès, et jeta des regards tristes sur le spectacle que présentait alors cette salle, où, la surveille, il avait vu tournoyer, emportées par la valse, les têtes des deux jeunes filles et des trois jeunes gens. Il frémit en pensant que dans peu elles devaient rouler tranchées par le sabre du bourreau. Attachés sur leurs fauteuils dorés, le père et la mère, les trois enfants et les deux filles, restaient dans un état d'immobilité complète. Huit serviteurs étaient debout, les mains liées derrière le dos. Ces quinze personnes se regardaient gravement, et leurs yeux trahissaient à peine les sentiments qui les animaient. Une résignation profonde et le regret d'avoir échoué dans leur entreprise se lisaient sur quelques fronts. Des soldats immobiles les gardaient en respectant la douleur de ces cruels ennemis. Un mouvement de curiosité anima les visages quand Victor parut. Il donna l'ordre de délier les condamnés, et alla lui-même détacher les cordes qui retenaient Clara prisonnière sur sa chaise. Elle sourit tristement. L'officier ne put s'empêcher d'effleurer les bras de la jeune fille, en admirant sa chevelure noire, sa taille souple. C'était une véritable Espagnole : elle avait le teint espagnol, les yeux espagnols, de longs cils recourbés, et une prunelle plus noire que ne l'est l'aile d'un corbeau.

– Avez-vous réussi ? dit-elle en lui adressant un de ces sourires funèbres où il y a encore de la jeune fille.

Victor ne put s'empêcher de gémir. Il regarda tour à tour les trois frères et Clara. L'un, et c'était l'aîné, avait trente ans. Petit, assez mal fait, l'air fier et dédaigneux, il ne manquait pas d'une certaine noblesse dans les manières, et ne paraissait pas étranger à cette délicatesse de sentiment qui rendit autrefois la galanterie espagnole si célèbre. Il se nommait Juanito. Le second, Philippe, était âgé de vingt ans environ. Il ressemblait à Clara. Le dernier avait huit ans. Un peintre aurait trouvé dans les traits de Manuel un peu de cette constance romaine que David a prêtée aux enfants dans ses pages républicaines. Le vieux marquis avait une tête couverte de cheveux blancs qui semblait échappée d'un tableau de Murillo. À cet aspect, le jeune officier hocha la tête, en désespérant de voir accepter par un de ces quatre personnages le marché du général ; néanmoins il osa le confier à Clara. L'Espagnole frissonna d'abord, mais elle reprit tout à coup un air calme et alla s'agenouiller devant son père.

– Oh ! lui dit-elle, faites jurer à Juanito qu'il obéira fidèlement aux ordres que vous lui donnerez, et nous serons contents.

La marquise tressaillit d'espérance ; mais quand, se penchant vers son mari, elle eut entendu l'horrible confidence de Clara, cette mère s'évanouit. Juanito comprit tout, il bondit comme un lion en cage. Victor prit sur lui de renvoyer les soldats, après avoir obtenu du marquis l'assurance d'une soumission parfaite. Les domestiques furent emmenés et livrés au bourreau, qui les pendit. Quand la famille n'eut plus que Victor pour surveillant, le vieux père se leva.

– Juanito ! dit-il.

Juanito ne répondit que par une inclinaison de tête qui équivalait à un refus, retomba sur sa chaise, et regarda ses parents d'un oeil sec et terrible. Clara vint s'asseoir sur ses genoux, et, d'un air gai : – Mon cher Juanito, dit-elle en lui passant le bras autour du cou et l'embrassant sur les paupières ; si tu savais combien, donnée par toi, la mort me sera douce. Je n'aurai pas à subir l'odieux contact des mains d'un bourreau. Tu me guériras des maux qui m'attendaient, et... mon bon Juanito, tu ne me voulais voir à personne, eh ! bien ?

Ses yeux veloutés jetèrent un regard de feu sur Victor, comme pour réveiller dans le coeur de Juanito son horreur des Français.

– Aie du courage, lui dit son frère Philippe, autrement notre race presque royale est éteinte.

Tout à coup Clara se leva, le groupe qui s'était formé autour de Juanito se sépara ; et cet enfant, rebelle à bon droit, vit devant lui, debout, son vieux père, qui d'un ton solennel s'écria : – Juanito, je te l'ordonne !

Le jeune comte restant immobile, son père tomba à ses genoux. Involontairement, Clara, Manuel et Philippe l'imitèrent. Tous tendirent les mains vers celui qui devait sauver la famille de l'oubli, et semblèrent répéter ces paroles paternelles : – Mon fils, manquerais-tu d'énergie espagnole et de vraie sensibilité ? Veux-tu me laisser longtemps à genoux, et dois-tu considérer ta vie et tes souffrances ? Est-ce mon fils, madame ? ajouta le vieillard en se retournant vers la marquise.

– Il y consent ! s'écria la mère avec désespoir en voyant Juanito faire un mouvement des sourcils dont la signification n'était connue que d'elle.

Mariquita, la seconde fille, se tenait à genoux en serrant sa mère dans ses faibles bras ; et, comme elle pleurait à chaudes larmes, son petit frère Manuel vint la gronder. En ce moment l'aumônier du château entra, il fut aussitôt entouré de toute la famille, on l'amena à Juanito. Victor, ne pouvant supporter plus longtemps cette scène, fit un signe à Clara, et se hâta d'aller tenter un dernier effort auprès du général ; il le trouva en belle humeur, au milieu du festin, et buvant avec ses officiers, qui commençaient à tenir de joyeux propos.

Une heure après, cent des plus notables habitants de Menda vinrent sur la terrasse pour être, suivant les ordres du général, témoins de l'exécution de la famille Léganès. Un détachement de soldats fut placé pour contenir les Espagnols, que l'on rangea sous les potences auxquelles les domestiques du marquis avaient été pendus. Les têtes de ces bourgeois touchaient presque les pieds de ces martyrs. À trente pas d'eux, s'élevait un billot et brillait un cimeterre. Le bourreau était là en cas de refus de la part de Juanito. Bientôt les Espagnols entendirent, au milieu du plus profond silence, les pas de plusieurs personnes, le son mesuré de la marche d'un piquet de soldats et le léger retentissement de leurs fusils. Ces différents bruits étaient mêlés aux accents joyeux du festin des officiers comme naguère les danses d'un bal avaient déguisé les apprêts de la sanglante trahison. Tous les regards se tournèrent vers le château, et l'on vit la noble famille qui s'avançait avec une incroyable assurance. Tous les fronts étaient calmes et sereins. Un seul homme, pâle et défait, s'appuyait sur le prêtre, qui prodiguait toutes les consolations de la religion à cet homme, le seul qui dût vivre. Le bourreau comprit, comme tout le monde, que Juanito avait accepté sa place pour un jour. Le vieux marquis et sa femme, Clara, Mariquita et leurs deux frères vinrent s'agenouiller à quelques pas du lieu fatal. Juanito fut conduit par le prêtre. Quand il arriva au billot, l'exécuteur, le tirant par la manche, le prit à part, et lui donna probablement quelques instructions. Le confesseur plaça les victimes de manière à ce qu'elles ne vissent pas le supplice. Mais c'était de vrais Espagnols qui se tinrent debout et sans faiblesse.

Clara s'élança la première vers son frère. – Juanito, lui dit-elle, aie pitié de mon peu de courage ! commence par moi !

En ce moment, les pas précipités d'un homme retentirent. Victor arriva sur le lieu de cette scène. Clara était agenouillée déjà, son cou blanc appelait le cimeterre. L'officier pâlit, mais il trouva la force d'accourir.

– Le général t'accorde la vie si tu veux m'épouser, lui dit-il à voix basse.

L'Espagnole lança sur l'officier un regard de mépris et de fierté.

– Allons, Juanito, dit-elle d'un son de voix profond.

Sa tête roula aux pieds de Victor. La marquise de Léganès laissa échapper un mouvement convulsif en entendant le bruit ; ce fut la seule marque de sa douleur.

– Suis-je bien comme ça, mon bon Juanito ? fut la demande que fit le petit Manuel à son frère.

– Ah ! tu pleures, Mariquita ! dit Juanito à sa soeur.

– Oh ! oui, répliqua la jeune fille. Je pense à toi, mon pauvre Juanito, tu seras bien malheureux sans nous.

Bientôt la grande figure du marquis apparut. Il regarda le sang de ses enfants, se tourna vers les spectateurs muets et immobiles, étendit les mains vers Juanito, et dit d'une voix forte : – Espagnols, je donne à mon fils ma bénédiction paternelle ! Maintenant, *marquis*, frappe sans peur, tu es sans reproche.

Mais quand Juanito vit approcher sa mère, soutenue par le

confesseur : – Elle m'a nourri ! s'écria-t-il.

Sa voix arracha un cri d'horreur à l'assemblée. Le bruit du festin et les rires joyeux des officiers s'apaisèrent à cette terrible clameur. La marquise comprit que le courage de Juanito était épuisé, elle s'élança d'un bond par-dessus la balustrade, et alla se fendre la tête sur les rochers. Un cri d'admiration s'éleva. Juanito était tombé évanoui.

– Mon général, dit un officier à moitié ivre, Marchand vient de me raconter quelque chose de cette exécution, je parie que vous ne l'avez pas ordonnée...

– Oubliez-vous, messieurs, s'écria le général G...t...r, que, dans un mois, cinq cents familles françaises seront en larmes, et que nous sommes en Espagne ? Voulez-vous laisser nos os ici ?

Après cette allocution, il ne se trouva personne, pas même un sous-lieutenant, qui osât vider son verre.

Malgré les respects dont il est entouré, malgré le titre d'*El verdugo* (le bourreau) que le roi d'Espagne a donné comme titre de noblesse au marquis de Léganès, il est dévoré par le chagrin, il vit solitaire et se montre rarement. Accablé sous le fardeau de son admirable forfait, il semble attendre avec impatience que la naissance d'un second fils lui donne le droit de rejoindre les ombres qui l'accompagnent incessamment.

Paris, octobre 1829.

Milton Keynes UK
Ingram Content Group UK Ltd.
UKHW050628301023
431584UK00009B/487